CREATING A HO

INTERIOR
DESIGN IDEAS

WARD LOCK

CONTENTS

A WARD LOCK BOOK

First published in the UK in 1997
by Ward Lock, Wellington House, 125 Strand,
London WC2R 0BB

A Cassell imprint

Copyright © Eaglemoss Publications Ltd 1997
Based on *Creating a Home*
Copyright © cover design Ward Lock 1997

Distributed in Australia
by New Holland Publishers Pty Ltd, 3/2 Aquatic Drive,
Frenchs Forest, NSW, Australia 2086

Distributed in Canada
by Cavendish Books Inc., Unit 5, 801 West 1st Street,
North Vancouver, B.C. Canada V7P 1PH

A British Library Cataloguing in Publication Data block for
this book may be obtained from the British Library

ISBN 0 7063 7652 8
Printed in Spain by Cayfosa Industria Grafica

10 9 8 7 6 5 4 3 2 1

INTRODUCTION

Creating a stylish room scheme takes careful selection of furniture, accessories and decorative treatments for walls and woodwork. Interior decorators spend years learning this skill, and charge highly for their services. This book shows you how to do it for yourself.

Interior Design Ideas is full of rooms of every type, from grand living rooms to tiny kitchens, furnished and decorated in the major decorative styles. Each chapter analyses one style, and examples of typical furniture and accessories with sample boards showing fabrics and wallcoverings, pinpoint its essential details.

The styles illustrated are rich and varied. From the 18th, 19th and early 20th centuries come the elegant English country house style, the more formal Georgian style, cluttered and cosy Victoriana, followed by the spacious, airy look of the Edwardian period. For country lovers there is cottage style, suitably adapted for urban living, and the rather more grand farmhouse style. Modernists have the whole of the 20th century to choose from. There's soft modern, the universally popular look featuring pastel colours and comfortable furniture; city modern, hard-edged, black and white, with hints of art deco; classic blond Scandinavian; the neo-thirties look; and the ultra-elegant, sometimes futuristic Italian look. Two more looks are based on materials: the leather library look, and decorating with classic English floral chintz fabrics.

Finally, a reference section illustrates furniture styles typical of the last four centuries, right up to present-day designs.

Interior Design Ideas will help you to achieve the look you want, whether you prefer a modern or traditional style of decor, for your whole house or for individual rooms.

Soft Modern

Up-to-date and streamlined as it is, Soft Modern is the essence of comfort. It's a light airy look by day that is transformed by subdued lighting – lots of shaded table lamps and candles, no overhead lights – into a warm atmospheric look at night time. This is a style that suits almost any type of home, whether old or new. Architectural details are unimportant because you can use wallpaper borders in place of non-existent features – at dado or picture-rail height, for example.

Colours are predominantly pastels –

sometimes almost bleached out; at other times warmer but still subdued, like dusty pink. They are used with small amounts of earthy shades and stronger accents.

Patterns are mixed with patterns, but they are soft and blurred so that nothing clashes. Traditional motifs such as chevrons, checks and trellises, live happily side by side with abstract designs that imitate textures and small smudgy florals.

Subtle fabrics are used in profusion – on windows as well as for upholstery.

Tailored roman blinds look neat but generous. So do the simple curtains that hang straight or are held with tiebacks.

Walls are covered with papers of gently patterned designs. Or they are painted in soft shades using the popular techniques of ragging, dragging and sponging. Woodwork, too, is often subjected to this subtle treatment. Fireplaces are generally painted. Ceilings are invariably white to increase the feeling of space and light, while the floors are close-carpeted or of light-coloured wood.

Finishing touches are stylish too: ceramics with crackle glazes, rounded shapes or strangely angled; table lamps with big conical shades; vases of tall blooms; tailored cushions trimmed with piping; pale rag rugs.

Silent night
Comfortable and welcoming on a winter's night, this room is just as appealing in daytime when the curtains are drawn back – sunlight softens the strong pink of the chairs and makes the room seem light and fresh.

▷ **Kitchen – light and sure**
Gentle colour with wood is the very essence of the Soft Modern look. White appliances and glass-fronted cupboards emphasize the feeling of light and space, and accessories repeat the pink and wood theme.

▽ **Bathroom softly dappled**
Smudged blue and pale green tiles are divided by a dado rail, woodwork is drag-painted, the blind is splashed with gentle colour.

▷ **Bedroom – comfort and joy**
A bedroom designed for comfort and relaxation. The walls and furniture have been kept very plain – interest focuses on the patchwork quilt, while the white-framed mirror behind the bed creates an illusion of space in a smallish room.

△ **Bathroom – luxury looks**
Although this elegant bathroom is large enough for a standard tub, using a corner bath means it feels more spacious – and looks luxurious. Classic floor tiles in soft and darker grey are a practical choice, and the introduction of pink in the floor-length curtains softens the overall effect.

△ **Bedroom – rhapsody in blue**
Masses of fabric around the windows and the bed in soft blue and white give a light, fresh look to this lovely bedroom. The patchwork quilt echoes the blue theme and adds a touch of pink. The long sweeping curtains are held back with ties for an almost theatrical effect – they give great style to what are, in reality, quite narrow windows.

The four-poster is a worthy centre-piece. You can build your own by boxing in a divan base and adding a frame of 5cm square posts. Position curtain tracks behind the frame at the top and hang with lightweight curtains, like these fine cotton striped ones.

◁ **Living room – pink and patterned**
The mixture of patterns in this stylish living room works because the colours are well co-ordinated and no one pattern is too dominant. The dark-stained occasional tables add interest, while the combination of long curtains and roman blinds shade the room from bright daylight.

ELEMENTS OF STYLE

This green and blue room is a perfect example of the Soft Modern style. It is simple and stunningly elegant.

Look at the features pointed out here and consider them when decorating in this style. Examine the photographs on the previous pages, too. Although each room is different, there is a very obvious common feel – the way the walls are treated, the kind of accessories, the type of furniture and fabrics, and most of all the use of colour and pattern.

It's a good idea to keep in mind how the room will look at night. Use subdued lighting – table lamps with big shades are good choices.

Window treatment
A roman blind is combined with a long draped curtain to elegant effect. The curtain is easy to make. Attach the curtain to the pole with Sew 'n' Stick Velcro (apply it using the method given on page 12). You may have to twist the fabric to the front so the right side is showing – the curtain will hang better if a lightweight fabric is used.

Walls
A soft, blurred wallpaper blends perfectly with the other patterns in the room. Co-ordination is an important feature of the Soft Modern style.

Picture rail
The picture rail is painted white with a wallpaper border below for added emphasis

Accessories
Ceramics play a supporting role – choose rounded shapes, strangely angled ones and box shapes. They should be highly glazed, perhaps with a crackle finish.

Furniture
The sofa and the tables are streamlined – fussy curves and flourishes are inappropriate. The light wood used for the tables suits the other elements in the room – dark wood needs a warmer colour scheme, such as the one on page 17.

Accents
Add interest with accents of stronger or contrasting colours. Here the green cushion and blue chair are very much in harmony with the rest of the scheme, the pink on the flower jug makes a pretty finishing touch.

Pastels and patterns
A mixture of patterns in soft pastel colours – such as pink, apricot and blue – in fabrics and wall coverings, combine with simple streamlined furniture and accessories to epitomize the Soft Modern look.

Here, patterns are mixed in fabrics with colours that blend perfectly; a small area of strong orange acts as an accent, in an otherwise pastel scheme.

A simple coffee table with a pale, wood laminate finish, round ceramic vases and table lamps, which cast a gentle light, are all finishing touches which contribute to the look.

DRAPED CURTAINS

This is a very easy method of making draped curtains. It is suitable for reversible fabrics such as plain or woven cottons, muslin and sheers.

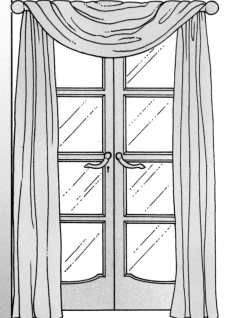

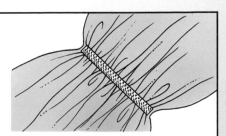

☐ Fix the curtain pole in position above the window. Measure for the fabric using a length of string: from the floor, draped over the pole at each end and down to the floor on the opposite side. Adjust until you get an attractive drape. Add an allowance for two double 5cm hems.

☐ The curtain is made from a single width, so choose a 122cm or wider fabric. You will also need a length of Sew 'n' Stick Velcro the width of the fabric. Stitch the hems at each end and press.

☐ Hang the fabric over the pole and arrange the drapes into attractive folds. Mark positions for Velcro slightly behind where the fabric passes over the pole at each end.

☐ Take down the fabric and, at both positions, sew two rows of gathering stitches across the fabric width and pull up evenly to half the fabric width. Fasten off. Stitch across gathers to hold in position. Cut the Velcro in half and stitch the 'sew' half over the gathering stitches on the wrong side.

☐ Apply self-adhesive half of Velcro to the curtain pole at the correct positions. Hang curtains over the pole and press the Velcro together.

▽ **Touches of style**
Look out for accessories to complete this streamlined look. Elegant glasses, such as these champagne flutes, china in simple shapes and pastel colours with linear decoration, and stipple-patterned ceramic tiles for the bathroom, are perfect finishing touches.

City Modern

A look of stark contrasts, City Modern is based on monochromatic (single-colour) schemes. It is best suited to urban living.

A combination of streamlined styles from both past and present, the furniture and accessories for the City Modern look are primarily angular in shape. At the window, venetian blinds or tailored roman blinds are the most suitable. They still let light enter while maintaining privacy and allowing the window area to remain as plain as possible.

Colours too are functional, being predominantly black or grey, with chrome trimmings on the furniture.

Accent colour is kept to a minimum, often seen in simply-shaped vases that are carefully placed, or large abstract prints hung on the wall.

Furniture has clearly defined edges with minimal detailing. Cabinets are either glass-fronted to show off the contents – a few pieces of ceramic or chrome objects – or plain-fronted to hide away any clutter.

Dining tables are clean-looking, stained, often with metal legs. Tablecloths are abandoned in favour of showing the stained – often black – wood and clear lines of the table itself.

Upholstered furniture should be con-fined to sofas which are long, low-backed and covered in neutral colours such as grey or black. There are few armchairs: two or more sofas are pre-ferred, with the occasional tubular chrome and leather chair.

Lighting is an important aspect of this look as it must be both decorative and functional. Floor and table lamps have a 1930s feel, as do simple chrome stan-dard lamps. Wall lights are used to create a softer atmosphere – which is essential when furniture and accessories are often so stark in outline.

Accessories are kept to a minimum: a ceramic vase holding tall flowers such as tulips or arum lilies, or a dramatic leafy plant. Chrome kitchenware ties in with tubular steel furniture.

Smart and sophisticated, this style is strongly defined and uncompromising. Its uncluttered lines are ideal for city flats, where space is so often at a premium.

▽ *Living room – city slick*
Classic chrome and leather chairs feature strongly, tying in with the tubular trolley. Lilies in a speckled vase fill the period fireplace, giving it a distinctly up-dated look.

▷ **Bedroom – cool and fresh**
The gentle curve of the grey bed frame,
highly reminiscent of the 1930s, is
echoed by the desk light. The plain
white of storage units that hide all the
clutter is relieved by simple grey
handles. The lightly geometric-
patterned wallpaper makes a suitable
background for the contemporary
prints that form a focal point in the
room. Simple grey-edged yellow
bedlinen adds a touch of freshness.

▽ **Living area – comfortably functional**
Pale grey is a slightly softer option for
walls if white looks too clinical. Here the
venetian blinds help to block out a dull
view. Accent colour is provided by
turquoise box files on the shelving unit,
while shiny black vases – in or out of use
– add an extra dimension. Tall flowers
in a pale floor vase and a large leafy
house plant help to soften this living
area's otherwise strict functionalism.

▽ Kitchen – sophisticated style

Plain dove grey kitchen units are given added interest by the ridged door surfaces in this very stylish, compact kitchen. The stainless steel cooker hood, oven front, saucepans and swivel chair at the breakfast bar provide shiny accents. Marble-look floor tiles carry smooth city sophistication through the entire room.

◁ Hallway – stunning entry

This interesting interpretation of a period hallway has combined original features with the City Modern look. The 19th century fireplace and mouldings have been retained and the area below the dado has been ragged. Rather than laying the standard chequerboard pattern, tiles have been used to form stripes. Thirties-inspired wall lights replace overhead pendants and a gallery of black and white photographs hangs along the wall, making a striking and thoroughly modern feature.

CITY SLICKER

This is a look that is surprisingly easy to create, featuring clear, simple lines in both furniture and accessories. Window treatments are also unfussy, with blinds or tailored curtains that can be used to block out an uninspiring view.

Lighting
Decorative as well as functional, atmosphere is all-important. Wall lights replace overhead pendants, while floor and freestanding lamps have shapes often reminiscent of the 30s.

Windows
Simplicity is the keynote here – blinds are roman, roller, or venetian, while curtains have a sophisticated tailored look, devoid of fussy detailing.

Furniture
Stained black ash features throughout the house. Detailing is kept to a minimum – coffee tables and dining furniture are often angular and have a streamlined look. Sofas and other upholstered furniture are covered in plain fabrics or leather.

Accessories
Choose cocktail glasses with a 30s feel, chrome kitchenware, speckled ceramics and elegantly-shaped tall vases. Accent colours are few. Yellow, dusky pink, cobalt blue, turquoise, bright green and red are all suitable, but use sparingly.

Walls
Wallpaper is light in tone with fine geometric patterns or stripes. As an alternative walls can be painted in white, cream or pale grey emulsion. Paintwork is also in neutral colours – and there should be no decorative dados or mouldings.

Flooring
Neutral colours predominate, and rugs with geometric designs provide interest to main rooms. Vinyl flooring suits this look if polished floorboards aren't an option.

△ Furniture

Furniture is black or grey. Stained ash tables, shelving and cupboards; simple but strong lines. Leather is the ideal upholstery material, not only for sofas but also for occasional and dining chairs. Combined with gleaming chrome, it typifies the City Modern look.

◁ Surfaces

Fabric designs are monochromatic and angular to tie in with the look.

Vinyl tiles – that can be laid in chequerboard or other patterns – and linoleum in speckled patterns cover areas where bare floorboards are unsuitable. Cream and grey can be used as alternative flooring colours to black and white. Plain walls suit this look and wallpaper should be used sparingly.

▷ *Accessories*

Small accessories are few in the City Modern flat as the look is essentially sleek, smart and uncluttered. Choose 30s-inspired objects: black lacquer picture frames, shiny chrome kitchenware and stainless steel utensils. Ceramics should be highly glazed and smooth, in simple shapes and either black or white, or softly coloured for accent.

▽ *Essentials*

Large floor-vases in dramatic black, or vivid Mediterranean hues for bright accent colour, are essential accessories for any room. Speckled bowls and vases tie in with flooring and cushions. Floor-standing lamps also act as decorative objects, reflecting the influence of the 30s on this look. Venetian blinds, if used, should be fine and can provide another opportunity for colour. But keep principally to black and white for a successful City Modern look.

Country Comes to Town

For city dwellers who choose the country look as the inspiration for decorating their homes, the country cottage model is not always a suitable choice. The scale of town houses often makes it difficult to recreate the cosiness of a small country retreat, particularly if the rooms lack any interesting features, and if the ceilings are high, or the windows are large, for instance.

This modern style captures some of the nostalgic atmosphere of the country cottage look, but it feels more sophisticated. It has touches of stripped pine in furniture and flooring, restrained colours in fabrics and wallcoverings, and collections of all sorts of china making a comfortable look which is easy and relaxing to live with.

COLOUR AND PATTERN

Country colours tend to be soft, and include not only the pretty pinks and fresh greens of the country cottage, but warm buttery yellows, cooled down with shades of blue. Matt or silk finish paints are the most suitable for walls and woodwork – such as tongued-and-grooved panelling – because they are close to the old finishes.

Patterned wallcoverings play a part in this look, too. Small geometrics are more suitable than tiny sprig designs which belong to the small scale of the country cottage style and would look lost on large walls. Stencilled borders – simple floral garlands, for example – or decorative paper borders add a touch of the countryside to a room scheme.

CHOOSING THE FURNITURE

Modern pine furniture with a plainer more streamlined outline mixes well with more traditional pieces; but don't go overboard with the stripped pine look, mix wooden with upholstered or painted furniture.

Cane and wicker furniture would be good choices too, either natural or painted to create a slightly more sophisticated look.

Dining room – simple elegance
A dining table with a mixture of different chairs does not suit this style. Here, the table, ladder-back chairs and corner cupboard are in a matching Victorian country style. The sprig wallpaper in a subtle mixture of colours has been carefully chosen to suit the scale of the room.

◁ **Bathroom – soft washes**
This traditional bathroom is painted in a sophisticated colour scheme of pinks and greys. Notice how the dado is blended into the overall wall colour rather than picked out in a different colour in the usual country style. A pinkish-grey carpet adds a luxurious finishing touch, topped with a dhurrie in deep pink, grey and jade stripes.

◁◁ **Elegant displays**
This Victorian-style pine cupboard, with attractive glass arched panels, makes an elegant alternative to the more familiar country dressers. A collection of glass is displayed inside and all sorts of jugs – some Victorian, some from the 1920s – are perched on top.

◁ **Living room – in the pink**
Deep pink is typical of the soft tones which suit this town and country look. Simple wooden furniture, a comfortable modern sofa and a Victorian-style tub chair create a relaxed feel to the room. The collection of watercolour landscapes and still life paintings, and the stone jar filled with flowers are perfect finishing touches.

▷ **Dining room – painted cane**
The natural materials of the country look are combined in an unusual way in this stylish kitchen/dining room. The cane dining table and chairs have been painted green to match the colour scheme in the kitchen. The wall is divided by a dado rail and the skirting boards are stripped and varnished. The polished wood floor gives a highly finished look to the room.

▽ **Kitchen – a flowery touch**
Pretty floral curtains, matching cushion covers and decorative border in autumn colours set the tone of this country-style kitchen. Delicate shades of cream and blue are used for the walls and also for the attractive tongued-and-grooved panelled dado.

△ **Bedroom – well co-ordinated**
Mini-print wallpaper and matching
fabrics for the curtains and bedcover
are the perfect partners for the
traditional pine furniture in this
bedroom. The chest of drawers is
probably mid-Victorian with a little
decorative beading around the drawers
and glass knobs. A large jug and bowl
with a floral design, and a vase of fresh
flowers complete the rural look.

Notice how a painted dado rail has
been added to create a more rustic feel
to the room.

▷ **Window dressing**
A combination of café curtains, which
cover the lower half of the window, and
simple, short curtains gives these large
windows a country look. The lemon
yellow fabric with a tiny sprig design is
edged with a frill and tied back with a
matching ribbon.

Traditional Elegance

Traditional Elegance harks back to the 18th century and the golden age of craftsmanship and design in Britain. During that period interiors were designed as frameworks for social events, and this style is still best suited to principal rooms. Proportions are important. If your home has large windows, high ceilings, and original features, this style is for you.

Often, the fireplace is the focal point of a room: a white marble Adam-type surround, with steel fender and grate, is still one of the most elegant styles to be found. A mirror or family portrait hangs above the fireplace, which can be filled with a flower arrangement.

Walls should be kept in pale background colours: blue, lemon, green or grey. Various painting techniques are well suited to this style, in particular ragging, dragging and marbling. Papers that echo these techniques are widely available. Alternatively, hang a paper with a discreet 'regency' stripe or tiny print, or one of the oriental-style designs known as 'chinoiserie'.

Windows are given a formal treatment: swags and tails or other elaborate headings, fringed or frilled curtains with heavy cord-and tassel tiebacks.

Fabrics Large, often stylized florals or stripes are usual for curtains or loose covers; damasks or brocades serve for upholstery as well as curtains.

Floors can be polished wood with large, traditionally-patterned rugs. These days fitted carpets in discreet background colours are more common.

Lighting, too, is unobtrusive: wall lights, chandeliers in the main rooms, and ceramic table lamps with pleated silk or chintz lampshades all suit this style. On dining tables and sideboards silver candelabra lend atmosphere.

Traditional Elegance is exactly as it sounds — a sophisticated look which is perfectly suitable for town or country life.

Bedroom – pretty relaxing
Large floral-design frilled curtains have a single swag secured at either end with a bow. The mix of antiques and easy furniture makes this room ideal for relaxing as well as sleeping.

△ **Drawing room – muted elegance**
An elegant yet comfortably informal drawing room in pale, muted tones is lifted by the use of a vibrant blue. The large floral arrangement that fills the Adam-style fireplace when not in use and the symmetrically-hung pictures on either side are typical of this style. It is apparent, too, in the pretty window treatment with its interesting but unfussy pelmet and the choice of furniture that includes comfortable armchairs and sofas with antiques or good reproduction pieces.

▷ **Bathroom – formal and light**
The pale geometric-patterned wallpaper and roller-blind fabric, coupled with the very stylized window treatment, give this luxurious bathroom a rather formal air. The bath panels have been marblized to tie in with the real marble splash-back and surround. Edwardian taps and modern brass accessories work well with the pale marble, adding to the air of Traditional Elegance.

BRIGHT IDEA

Dress up a chair that needs re-upholstering by making a cushion from 5cm foam, cut to shape and boxed in a suitable fabric. Pipe the cushion with cord and make cord ties to secure the cushion to the chair back. Attach tassels to each cord end – four in all. Allow plenty of cord and large tassels.

△ *Hallway – discreetly striped*
This classic cream-and-gold treatment of hall and stairway shows how well the style adapts to a small town house. Discreet striped wallpaper is often associated with the Regency period and certainly suits this hall with its huge flower arrangement on the console and ornate gilt-framed mirror above. Careful attention has been paid to detail – the marble effect of the floor tiles has been extended to the skirting, with the colours repeated in the dado rail.

▷ *Sitting room – classical warmth*
The somewhat imposing proportions of this room are lessened by the use of warm apricot tones throughout. Brown and apricot-patterned curtains have a traditional swag-and-tail heading and the relief design on the painted fire surround is picked out in crisp white. A collection of family portraits is hung over the fireplace in classic style and prized ornaments displayed along the mantelpiece. Task lighting is provided by elegant table lamps. The furniture arrangement of comfortable sofa and armchairs forming two sides of a square and focusing on the fireplace makes the seating area the centrepiece of the room – ideal for easy conversation.

Accessories

Large carved and gilded mirrors hung over a mantelpiece or sideboard suit almost any room; prints and portraits also hang on the wall or stand on occasional tables. Choose a few pieces of china and silver and place a huge floral arrangement on its own. For the dining table go for good china and glass in classic 18th-century styling.

Walls

Painted or papered in pale classic background colours; discreet stripes or chinoiserie patterns to provide a backdrop for elegant furniture and accessories. Woodwork, cornices, and relief work should be contrasting.

DINING IN STYLE

The room most likely to be decorated in a traditional manner is the dining room, as furnishings and accessories here are often inherited pieces. It tends, too, to be the most formal room in the house, less used by children and more for evening entertaining, and therefore allowing the display of china and glass either on a sideboard or in display cabinets.

Furniture

Antique or good reproduction pieces in mahogany, rosewood or walnut veneer, especially in the style of Chippendale, Sheraton or Hepplewhite. Comfortable sofas and easy chairs where appropriate.

Flooring

Fitted carpets are often best for town houses. Alternatively, choose a large carpet to lay over polished floorboards. A big-scale design with a strong border, often in muted colours, is ideal.

Soft furnishings

Windows are often elaborately dressed with pelmets and tiebacks. Use rich damasks and stripes for upholstery and formal drapes; large floral designs for bedroom and living room curtains.

◁ **Accessories**

This is not a cluttered style. Choose pieces whose design harks back to the 18th century, the 'golden age' of fine craftsmanship in Britain. Jasperware by Wedgwood with its classical relief work, elegantly shaped china, and silver candelabra and tableware all suit this traditional style.

▽ **Furniture**

The 18th century is the one to follow for furniture that is both traditional and elegant. The dining chair with Prince of Wales' feathers is in Hepplewhite style, while the lower, square-backed chair is characteristic of Sheraton. Above all, furniture should be distinctive, as is this sofa-table with brass handles and ormolu mounts.

△ Essentials

Brass reproduction light fittings are most suitable, though they don't give the atmospheric light of real candles. For living rooms and bedrooms choose porcelain lamp bases in classical shapes and add a pleated silk shade. Plenty of cushions, in stripes or large floral designs, co-ordinate with other soft furnishings.

▽ Fabrics and wallcoverings

Use damask for upholstery and curtains, or a large-scale floral design – especially if you want to make the most of a large window area. Chinoiserie for both walls and fabrics has been popular since tea arrived in England, and striped 'regency' wallpaper and fabric is very suitable for the traditional elegance of this look.

Classic English Floral Chintz

Indian chintz caused a sensation when it first arrived in Europe around 300 years ago. Seventeenth century bedrooms boasted chintz spreads, curtains and even chintz floorcloths. The name 'chintz', derives from the Hindi word 'chints', meaning painted or printed fabrics and now describes any cotton furnishing fabric with a predominantly floral pattern and glazed finish.

Colours and patterns Early stylized floral chintz was much influenced by European embroideries brought out for Indian artists to copy.

Traditional English chintz usually means old-fashioned, very realistic, floral designs of full-blown roses, parrot tulips, peonies, lilies and wild flowers; often incorporating other motifs such as ribbons and birds. Today's chintz style favours larger, less defined blossoms and mixes several different patterns.

Choosing the furnishings Generous, full-length chintz curtains look best with frilled edges and pelmets. Roman or austrian blinds in plain or all-over prints in glazed cotton also add extra elegance. Sofas and armchairs are traditional and comfortable with chintz or complementary plain or printed linen loose covers.

Other furniture is mainly mahogany in traditional styles; for a more modern feel mellow antique pine works well. Round tables made from chipboard can be covered with floor-length cloths of patterned chintz or glazed cotton. Coolie lampshades covered in chintz or wall fittings with decorative sconces suit this look. Walls can be covered with flowery papers or emulsion-painted for a plainer look. Floors can be bare boards covered with oriental rugs, or pastel fitted carpets.

Living room – quiet elegance
This typically lush mid-Victorian glazed chintz mixes perfectly with modern mock-moiré glazed cotton in the austrian blind and tablecloth.

◁ **Seating – modern looks**
By the end of the 18th century industrial fabric printing had resulted in more natural-looking floral patterns and colours, mostly on light backgrounds. Today's chintzes come in paint-box fresh simple florals with a huge choice of background colours. Here, cushions and loose covers blend harmoniously with a striped, glazed cotton, roman blind.

▽ **Bedroom – plain and patterned**
Plain walls and a neutral carpet on the floor balance the Jacobean-looking print in these chintz curtains, covered bedhead and divan base. A quiet trellis-patterned glazed cotton quilt co-ordinates well with the busy patterned chintz without being too insistent. The wall lamps have plain brackets to emphasize this plainer chintz look.

▽ *Co-ordinating patterns*
For an all-over chintz look try mixing patterns. Here, floral patterns in similar colours link the curtains and upholstery. A plain glazed cotton tablecloth is less busy than a floral chintz would be for this style.

△ **Living room – cottage**
A plain white-painted dado provides relief to the busy floral walls and matching chintz curtains. Muted reds in the Indian rug and cushion covers here blend perfectly with the bright pinks and reds in the fabric and wallpaper. The trompe l'oeil painted vase of flowers and cat add witty touches.

▷ *Sitting room – warm and practical*
Warm apricots and cream are a practical choice with dark flooring and walls. The result is a less flowery look and a sunny all-the-year-round feel to this seating arrangement

STYLING WITH CHINTZ

Classic chintz is an essentially comfortable look and at home in both town and country settings. Walls can be plain painted, or papered in small-scale trellis, florals or stripes; floral borders also help to emphasize the flowery chintz feeling.

Floorcoverings can be fitted carpets in neutral or pastel colours, or polished boards with oriental rugs. Lighting is atmospheric: table lamps with coolie shades of pleated chintz or silk shades in soft pastel colours. Wall lamps are either simple plaster candle bracket-and-shade fittings, or more ornate gilded sconces. Mix floral china in different patterns, fill china bowls with pot pourri to perfume the room. Plump, feather-filled cushions covered in different chintzes make essential accessories.

Lighting
For a traditional look choose silk shades in empire and panelled square shapes as decorative table lamps or wall lamps with candle holders and gilt sconces. Coolie shades covered in chintz with ginger jar bases give a more modern look.

Windows
Curtains should be generous and full, preferably with frilled pelmets and edges; grander windows can have decorative pelmets and tie-backs. Roman or austrian blinds can be in matching or co-ordinating chintzes – or plain glazed cottons.

Seating
Traditional-style comfortable sofas and armchairs, either upholstered or loose covered – often in serviceable linen union in a pattern that matches the chintz. Piping in a contrasting colour gives a tailored finish.

Furniture
A few good pieces of mahogany for chairs and tables, in 18th century and Victorian styles. Round chipboard tables can be covered with chintz or glazed cotton floor-length cloths and used to display family photos and fine china.

Flooring
Plain polished floorboards or fitted carpets in light and dark colours. Indian and Persian rugs in soft, muted colours go well with traditional chintz. Chinese cut-pile rugs with simple border patterns in pastel colours also look good.

Accessories
Pick traditional fine bone china in bright colours that emphasize the colours in the chintz. Choose plain ceramics and porcelain if you want to play down the floral effect.

▷ *Line and shape*
Wing-back chairs are normally upholstered in heavy, hard-wearing fabrics but the new, fresh chintzes give a softer, more feminine look that contrasts particularly well with dark wood side tables and comfortable upholstered stools.

▽ *Wallpapers and fabrics*
There is a lot of choice about in co-ordinating chintz-style wallpapers, borders and fabrics. To mix and match these successfully use patterns of different scales and contrast large exuberant rosy florals with trellis and small all-over prints.

△ **Accessories**
Pick Victorian bone china in bright colours and curvy shapes. Have pretty chintzy table linens in the dining room and floral boxes and bowls filled with pot pourri.

▽ **Essentials**
Chintz coolie shades have a modern feel; for traditional looks pick silk empire shades. Mix different chintz cushions with the occasional plain glazed cotton.

The Leather 'Library Look'

Think of country house libraries — rooms where you can pen a love letter, dream in front of an open fire on a wet afternoon, doze off under a newspaper; curl up on a comfortable old leather sofa with a night cap poured from a crystal decanter. Libraries are definitely rooms for relaxing — places for contemplation rather than action — and the furnishings reflect this.

Library influences also come from gentlemen's clubs with their well-polished heavy wooden furniture and floor-to-ceiling bookcases, often with beautiful glazed and leaded light fronts filled with beautifully bound leather books. Then there are deep, roomy leather armchairs trimmed with decorative brass studs that give both privacy and comfort. Brass is also much in evidence in fireside accessories and decorative lighting.

But perhaps the focal point of the traditional country house library is the Davenport-style desk with its tooled leather top. Charles Dickens sat in a smoker's chair at such a desk in his study at Gads Hill Place, where he wrote 'Great Expectations', 'Our Mutual Friend' and a 'Tale of Two Cities'.

PATTERN AND COLOUR

Pattern is mainly confined to walls, which may be covered with striped, flocked, or marbled papers — or dragged and sponged paint finishes in dark colours. Curtains and some upholstery may have tapestry, paisley or country-house chintz designs in rich glowing colours. Oriental rugs are also a feature and brighten plain wall-to-wall carpeting or plain polished floorboards. Colours are warm and inviting; soft rich reds, olive and bottle greens, deep sapphire blues — all the colours used traditionally in old craftsman-made leather book-bindings.

Study — warm and inviting
The classic library look: the rich colour of traditional yew wood furniture blends well with an antiqued red leather upholstered chair and plum fabric-covered walls. Dark, rich prints at the window also help this room to feel warm and comfortable.

◁ **Living room – masculine**
Book-lined alcoves and brown painted walls make this large room feel warm and inviting. The natural sisal carpet and the mirror above the mantelpiece which reflects the white ceiling and glossy walls help to lighten this dark sophisticated scheme.

▽ **Living room – feminine**
The library look can also be a feminine one. Here, striped wallpaper blends in with the soft geometric fabric of the curtains and tablecloths. The pleated skirts of the side tables and the full tailored curtains with their softly pleated swags contrast with the more formal tails and the largely plain upholstery fabrics.

MILITARY LOOK

Brass corner pieces, available at most DIY outlets, can be fixed to modern tables to imitate traditional campaign furniture which was protected by metal corners.

◁ *Study corner*
A group of horsy oil paintings hung symmetrically above a writing desk gives a living room corner the right air.

▽ *Bedroom – tailored look*
A tailored bedspread and strong colours gives this bedroom with its own study corner a comfortable, masculine feeling.

ACHIEVING THE LOOK

Bargains in genuine Regency and Victorian kneehole desks, bookcases and military furniture are scarce but good quality reproduction examples abound in yew, mahogany, and golden oak. Seating is mostly high-backed wing chairs or chesterfields upholstered in buttoned leather. Ideally, beautiful leather-bound books should be stored in glass-fronted bookcases to keep out the dust. But open shelves can be built into alcoves either side of a chimney breast and combined with neat cupboards below.

Windows should be dressed witn generous curtains or blinds that provide plenty of shade to protect prints and book bindings and give a luxurious warm look. Walls can be covered in dark papers or softly sponged. Good, soft lighting is also essential – decorative brass oil lamps fit the mood while shelves and bookcases can incorporate discreet built-in display lighting. Leather-trimmed accessories, racing or botanical prints and old maps add atmosphere. Handsome brass and leather club fenders and fire accessories make the fireplace a real focal point.

Mirrors
Large mirrors with elegant 18th century gilt mouldings suit this look and create an important focal point. Mirrors reflecting something light can also usefully brighten dark interiors and prevent them from feeling too gloomy and 'closed in'.

Accessories
Silver or gold-framed photographs, hunting prints and oil paintings, a brass carriage clock and heavy brass candlesticks look well on mantelpieces. Stylish writing accessories such as inkwells and blotters complete the look for writing desks.

Windows
Cover windows with heavy curtains which fall in rich folds, often to the floor. Plain roller blinds in a fabric to match the curtains add extra warmth.

Cabinet furniture
Choose pieces made from warm woods such as mahogany, yew and cherry. Furniture should be substantial and made to last – rolltop desks, writing bureaux and chests of drawers are characteristic and often have tooled leather tops.

Upholstered furniture
Comfortable, wing-backed armchairs and chesterfield sofas, upholstered in dark leather or velvet, often button-backed. Upholstered footstools and traditional smoker's chairs are also appropriate.

Lighting
Avoid overly bright, direct lighting – instead choose gentle background light. Traditional wall and ceiling fittings with unfussy table and standard lamps for pools of task lighting.

▽ **Line and shape**
Furniture is substantial, usually made of rich wood;
seating is upholstered in dark buttoned leather.
A brass upholstery tack trim is characteristic.

▽ **Fabrics and trimmings**
Combine dark, jewel-rich colours with luxurious
textures in velvet combined with flamestitch and
stylized floral cotton fabrics. Add thick fringes to
cushions and use heavy rope tiebacks for curtains.

◁ **Essentials**
Desk lamps with heavy, opaque shades throw a bright, concentrated pool of light which is characteristic of this look. Both the lamps shown here are adustable, to throw light exactly where it is needed. Wall brackets are also typical. Brass is an essential ingredient, so choose brass lamps, fenders and companion sets.

▽ **Accessories**
Most library accessories are functional as well as decorative. Crystal decanters, cigar and cigarette boxes, lighters and brass carriage clocks are all typical. Chess sets, card games and high-quality writing accessories, ranging from pen and pencil holders to decorative blotters, inkwells and antique-looking globes adorn desk tops.

Conservatory Style

You can successfully achieve the conservatory 'look' anywhere in the house by making your rooms feel like an extension of the garden – or even a substitute for one. The overall effect should be light and airy and if you don't have a room with lots of natural light, you can still create a fresh, outdoor look with the right choice of colours, fabrics and furniture.

Colours are soft pastels, creams and white with a generous amount of green – from dark emerald to olive, through to the palest leafy greens. Patterns are busy, colourful floral designs to imitate herbaceous borders or sprays of flowers, or trellis designs – use anything that gives a garden feel.

Walls can be treated simply as background for plants – painted or papered in plain, pale shades – or as substitutes for plants and covered in rambling floral design wallpapers.

If you plan to fill the rooms with plants, then use flooring that won't be damaged by water spills – quarry or ceramic tiles or less expensive vinyl are suitable, as is natural-look sisal or coir matting which feels warmer underfoot. Add rag rugs for extra comfort and warmth. If you do choose carpet, keep to natural shades.

Furniture has a summery, outdoor feel: wicker, bamboo and cane are ideal. White-painted wrought iron, though attractive, can be uncomfortable. Upholstered seating is not really in keeping with this style, so try instead a mass of cushions in mixed sizes and flowery patterns or bright, glowing plains.

Window treatments depend on the size and shape of your windows as well as the other furnishings in the room. Try split cane or bamboo blinds with natural furniture, or floral design curtains or roller blinds with plumpy cushions.

For lighting, choose basketware shades or glass globe wall lights on wrought iron supports. Uplighters hidden among plants show off the foliage.

Of course you'll need plenty of containers to hold the profusion of plants that is central to this look – and plenty of fresh flowers for a summery feeling all year round.

Conservatory bay
Large windows give an unrestricted view of the garden beyond, and large potted plants thrive in the light. Furniture is simply-shaped cane and bamboo, with comfortable cushions in a floral print.

▷ **Dining room – olive green**
The fresh white and green colour scheme gives a garden atmosphere that is emphasized by bamboo chairs with trellis-like framework. The chairs are stained to match the olive green carpet and seat cushions.

The darker green detailing on the panelled door is echoed by the trimming on the simple roman blinds. Bistro wall lights look perfect in this setting, while pale walls and tablecloth complete the garden feel.

▽ **Living room – botanical corner**
A feeling of the outdoor prevails in this beautiful sitting room. Furniture is grouped next to the large french windows. There are pots and vases containing masses of greenery, botanical prints hang over the table and wicker chair – and even the chair cushions are printed with pots of herbs.

△ **Bedroom – country-look**
Natural cane headboard and chair combine with softly-patterned wallpaper and fabrics to pretty effect. The pine dressing table has a stencilled design on each drawer.

△ **Dining room – flowery**
Busy, floral wallpaper
dominates this sunny dining
room where the pink on the
wall is picked out in the china
and cutlery. A bamboo blind
and plant holders match the
furniture and a thin louvre
door makes a feature of the
window.

◁ **Living room – all white**
Everything in this sunny
corner is painted white – the
walls and woodwork, the
cane furniture and plant
stand. The only colour and
decoration is in a delicate
floral border above the high
dado, and in the cushions and
accessories. Even the plants
in this peaceful garden-style
retreat are light and delicate.

GREEN AND PLEASANT

A major colour for this look is green – whether the clear green and white reminiscent of palm trees and foliage plants in a hot house/conservatory or the softer greens and gently-coloured blooms of an English country garden. If you can't have the real thing, then create your own indoor garden with colourful mixed floral-design wallpapers and fabrics.

Furniture and floorcoverings need to be kept as far as possible in natural materials and colours: cane or bamboo, for example. Trelliswork on the walls – either real or designed on wallpaper – adds to the garden room feeling and provides the perfect background for plants.

The finished overall effect is light and airy. Use as many pot plants and cut flowers as possible.

Plants
As many plants as possible, in terracotta, ceramic or basketware planters. You can vary their heights with jardinières or cane plant stands. Botanical prints or pictures with a summery feel are ideal, and vases of flowers and plain coloured cushions can be used to pick out accent colour from your floral fabrics.

Windows
Allow as much light in as possible. Louvred shutters give a dappled, summery effect. Bamboo, split cane or rice paper blinds are also suitable. For curtains, choose floral or trellis patterns.

Walls
Plain, pale walls reflect as much light as possible. Here they are off-white, but will work just as well in a pale green or peach. Wallpapers have flowery sprays or climbing roses, or trelliswork designs for a more formal look.

Fabrics
Florals are the best choice, in colours that are light and bright. A mixture of patterns imitates a summer herbaceous border. Plain cushions in bright, glowing colours act as accent points.

Flooring
Natural flooring looks best against wicker furniture. Sisal or coir matting is cheap and fairly hardwearing. Terracotta or ceramic tiles make your room look like a real conservatory but they can be cold underfoot; cover them with rugs. Carpet should be in natural shades.

Furniture
Has a garden or outdoor feel. Wicker, bamboo or cane are ideal, either left in their natural colour or painted in pastel colours. The glass top on the table in this picture makes it stable and thus ideal for serving drinks.

In the Georgian Manner

The Georgian era in the 18th century is considered by many to be one of the high points of British architecture and interior decoration. Inspired by the architecture of Greece and Rome, and fuelled by the growing prosperity of the age, this most English of styles de-veloped in houses with large rooms, high ceilings and tall windows. The Georgian style can, however, be adapted to suit well-proportioned modern rooms, and Georgian elements can be included in more modest homes.

The restrained and graceful style favoured by the Georgians depended on their almost infallible eye for pro-portion. Symmetry and balance were all-important: what happened on one side of a room was balanced by what happened on the other. The fireplace – generally classical in shape and flanked by paired columns – represented the clear focal point of a room and the recesses beside the chimney breast were decorated identically. Furniture and ornaments were carefully arranged.

Architecturally, Georgian rooms were usually divided into three sections with a dado towards the bottom of the walls and a fairly wide frieze and cornice near the top.

Walls Wallpaper was expensive in the 18th century and was rarely stuck directly on walls. Fabric, or paper pasted on to canvas, was mounted on battens with beading covering the joins.

Timber panelling (known as wains-coting) was cheaper than either fabric or paper. Hardwood panelling was usually left in its natural colour but cheaper deal or pine panelling was always painted – stripped pine is defi-nitely a late 20th-century fashion! Fitted furniture, however, is not a modern invention: cupboards were incorpor-ated within the panelling, as were display niches on either side of the fireplace.

Early in the 18th century, panelling was often completely painted in a shade of grey, brown, olive green, or off-white. Later, though, a wider and brighter palette became available – yellow, red, or sky blue were not unusual – and in some homes white or coloured plaster mouldings (formerly used only for cornices and friezes) were teamed with contrasting panels of paint, paper, or fabric.

Windows in drawing rooms often ex-tended almost from floor to ceiling. Twelve-pane sash windows (with six panes in each sash) were most typical. Fabric was expensive and was used fairly sparingly on windows. Elaborate swags and tails topped roman or austrian blinds or a single curtain was looped to one side.

Floors Flagstones or unpolished boards covered with rush or straw matting were most common. Carpets, which in previous centuries were hung on walls or draped over tables, made an appear-ance on the floors of grander houses and spread to less wealthy homes.

Drawing room – classical
This room abounds in classical features – a pedimented mirror, symmetrical alcoves flanking the fireplace, an elaborate cornice, and wall lights above a selection of miniatures.

FURNITURE AND FURNISHINGS

Mahogany furniture, chandeliers and candlesticks, and patterned fabrics characterize Georgian interior decor.

Furniture Georgian rooms were comparatively sparsely furnished with tables and chairs ranged around the walls; the dado (or chair) rail was there to protect the wallcovering.

The designs of the famous furniture-makers – Sheraton, Hepplewhite and Chippendale – typify Georgian taste in furniture. Although walnut was still used, the most popular wood was mahogany. Padded wing chairs with cabriole or straight legs were usual; armless, straight-backed upholstered chairs or stools made ideal seats for ladies wearing fashionably wide, hooped skirts. Coffee tables did not exist in the 18th century; their role was filled by drop-ended sofa tables and drop-sided Pembroke tables.

Lighting was provided entirely by candles or rush lights which, not surprisingly, were a major expense in the domestic budget! Chandeliers and decorative lanterns containing several candles became fashionable. Wall sconces were often backed with mirror for decoration and to reflect more light.

Fabrics and wallpapers Velvets and silk damasks were used in grand houses. Cottons, at first in simple block-printed designs, monochrome pastoral scenes (also used on walls) and, as techniques improved, colourful floral designs, were less expensive. Papers were plain, flocked, or decorated with flower and bird motifs in imitation of imported Chinese designs. There were also cheaper 'domino' prints with small geometric designs. Borders did not necessarily co-ordinate with the paper.

△ *Living room – the right mood*
Although this room lacks the architectural features of the Georgian era, it nevertheless has the correct feel. An evenly-matched arrangement of pieces of upholstered furniture is combined with a muted colour scheme.

▽ *Drawing room – symmetrical*
The symmetry which epitomizes the period is evidenced by the pair of windows, each of which is a mirror image of the other. The elaborate pelmet and simple treatment below are characteristic.

△ **Fireplace – uncluttered**
Choosing a wallpaper of the correct period helps set the mood in a Georgian room. The original fragment of this reproduction 'domino' print dates from around 1800 and was unearthed from below at least a dozen layers in a London house. Borders were commonly used to cover the edges where the paper was fixed to battens – this design dates from around 1780.

△ **Dining room – formal**
The Georgian look is particularly suitable for formal dining rooms. Deep blue wallpaper and fabric, together with Chippendale-style upholstered ladder-back chairs and lots of rich mahogany set off shiny silver candlesticks and crystal goblets to perfection.

◁ **Hallway – in character**
In a long and narrow entrance hall, Georgian simplicity of decor enhances the size of the space. Although the actual pieces of furniture themselves are not strictly typical of the period, the positioning of a pair of chairs flanking a mahogany bureau is typically Georgian. Note how the gilded mirror and two gilt-framed paintings echo the arrangement of the furniture.

ADAPTING THE STYLE

Creating a Georgian-style room need not be impossibly expensive, despite the fact that authentic Georgian furniture is costly and few people live in homes built during the period. Although large rooms are not essential, the style works best in spacious, high-ceilinged rooms. In less imposing homes, it's important to retain the Georgian sense of proportions – for instance, by not overloading a small room with the full complement of dado rail, cornice and frieze. Happily, many fabrics and papers of the period are made today. Keep elaborate or grand designs for large rooms and use small patterns elsewhere.

Coffee tables, so essential to modern life, did not exist in the 18th century. Instead, choose occasional furniture such as Pembroke or sofa tables. Large round library drum tables, with leather tops and alternate real and dummy drawers round the edge, were widely used; small modern adaptations of these tables make attractive side tables, and low versions can serve as coffee tables.

Walls
Plain, painted walls suit this style in either muted shades or the bright colours which became fashionable later in the century. Recreate the panelled look with painted or papered panels enclosed by plaster or wood mouldings or wallpaper borders.

Lighting
Lacking either electricity or gas, the Georgians relied on candles for domestic lighting. Ceiling-hung, candelabra-style fittings are suitable. Silver or brass candlesticks add a touch of authenticity.

Windows
Large windows, ideally reaching almost from floor to ceiling, are characteristic of Georgian architecture. Keep window coverings relatively simple – fabric was expensive in the 18th century!

Architectural details
A dado, frieze and cornice are essential ingredients of classic Georgian rooms. If your ceiling is not high enough for all three elements to work well, it is better to leave out one element. Perhaps a low dado and simple cornice, or a frieze and cornice but no dado.

Floors
Choose polished floorboards, wood-block or parquet flooring, or carpet the floor with sisal matting or a plain carpet in an unobtrusive colour. Add real oriental rugs, or modern copies, over any of these floorcoverings.

Furniture
Authentic Georgian antiques are expensive; instead look for Victorian or Edwardian copies or modern reproductions. Choose Hepplewhite, Chippendale and Sheraton styles for chairs and cabinet furniture, and upholstered wing chairs.

Fireplace
Reproduction Georgian fireplaces are widely available. Keep the style you choose in scale with your room. A large, ornate fireplace will be too dominant in a smallish room; instead choose a more modest and restrained design.

◁ **Essentials**
Although it is impractical to rely only on candlelight, as the Georgians did, choose electric fittings which look as if they were designed to be used with candles.

Traditional brass and glass chandeliers and pendant lanterns suit Georgian rooms. Look for modern versions of wall-hung lamps (sconces) with mirrored backs. Wall-mounted brass picture lights also have the right feeling for the period.

As well as real candles, choose table lamps with tall bases like candlesticks or classical columns.

▽ **Line and shape**
A fireplace with classically simple lines sets the style in a Georgian room..Choose substantial mahogany furniture and chairs with straight legs and ladder- or shield-backs; upholstered wing chairs also have the right period feel.

▷ **Accessories**
Look for copies of original Georgian silver:
this teapot was made in the 1930s and the
wine coaster is even newer. While
tableware was earthenware or porcelain,
modern floral china is acceptable. The white
jug and dish are copies of Georgian designs.

▽ **Surfaces**
Fabrics and wallpapers range
from simple block-printed
patterns to multi-coloured,
stylized designs and flowery
prints. Narrow wallpaper
borders in architectural patterns
and gilt fillets (edging strips) give
papered walls a panelled feel.
Traditional plaster mouldings are
still being made today.

Victorian Values

The Victorian era – the period between 1837 and 1901 – was a time of massive industrial development and this was reflected in people's homes. Factories started to mass produce items which previously only the wealthy could afford. Ornate furniture could be factory-made faster and at a lower cost than simple handmade pieces. With improved printing and weaving methods, patterned wallpapers and fabrics were used instead of paint and hand woven furnishing fabrics.

Colours and patterns of this style are distinctive. The Victorians were very keen on nature and this was reflected indoors. Floral patterns are used a lot, often in strong rich colours as well as prettier pastels.

The Orient was a strong influence, too – this was the height of the British Empire – and traditional designs from the East are used in rugs laid on polished boards or over carpet.

Windows are covered with heavy drapes, held back with tasselled tie-backs and often combined with decorative pelmets and floor-length lace panels.

Furniture ranges from the highly ornate to the more bulky and solid, preferably in dark woods. The original furniture is quite expensive but good reproductions are available.

There should be plenty of knick-knacks and pictures framed in dark wood and photographs in silver frames, patterned china and leather-bound books. And, of course, plants. No Victorian home would have been complete without at least one aspidistra.

Living room – old and new
A clever mix of furniture, fabrics and objects, centred by a pretty fireplace, gives this room an authentic air. The furnishings and the many ornaments provide the typical cluttered look.

△ **Bedroom – height of luxury**
Strongly patterned wallpaper and fabric
are hallmarks of the Victorian style.
In this bedroom the curtains are long
and generous to match the canopy over
the bed, and there are frilled cushions,
pictures and colourful knick-knacks in
silver and porcelain. The circular
bedside tables are covered with long
patterned cloths and glazed chintz over-
cloths. The screen, an item often seen in
19th century homes, is painted and
decorated with cards and some
interesting dolls' straw hats.

▷ **Kitchen – modern and traditional**
These days, a real Victorian kitchen,
with a large range and cook's pantry,
would not be very practical. But if you
incorporate modern technology into a
Victorian-style kitchen you can get the
best of both worlds. Here, new units
provide the necessary storage space
while the original fireplace, with a
selection of prints on the chimney
breast above, gives the room its period
character. The stained-glass window
and chequered floor tiles add an
authentic air.

◁ **Bathroom – typically tiled**
Original Victorian tiles are the focal
point of this tiny bathroom. Recurring
colours of rust, green and cream allow
the different patterns to work together.
A similar look can easily be created with
the wide range of reproduction tiles
available today. And it is still possible to
find old bathroom fittings with their
brass taps in working order.

△ **Living room – pattern**
The rich colours of sage
green, cream and brown in
the living room above were
frequently used in Victorian
homes. Plain coloured velvet
upholstery is the perfect foil
to the patterned wallpaper.
The original cast-iron
fireplace has been painted.
Plants complete the effect.

▷ **Dining room – in bloom**
In this dining room the pretty
floral wallpaper and matching
curtains provide a charming
contrast to the heavy
wooden furniture and create
a definite air of Victoriana.
The circular table can be
draped with a cloth and
covered with lace when not
being used.

ELEMENTS OF STYLE

This pretty bedroom combines many elements so typical of the Victorian period. The style is ornate but cosy and surfaces are covered with china, framed family photographs, leather-bound books, ornaments and other decorative accessories. China washing bowls and jugs on a mahogany washstand are typical.

In bedrooms dark woods are contrasted with attractive floral prints or stronger patterns. Curtains and bed linen are flounced and frilled with matching or contrasting material. Pattern and colour combine well when mixed, and bedlinen, curtains and tablecloths are often trimmed with lace.

Wall-mounted lights which give a warm and atmospheric tone are used in preference to central pendants. And note the abundance of pictures on the walls and the variety of different shaped frames. All this adds to the look.

Wallcovering
Highly patterned wallpaper in pretty floral colours as well as richer reds and blues for living rooms. For contrast a plain paper is often used below the dado or above the picture rail. Notice how the bed head, the valance and the quilt match the wallpaper.

Finishing touches
Accessories are vital for a period look. Cover walls with paintings, needlepoint and photographs in frames of differing shapes and sizes, and other surfaces with bric-a-brac. China water jugs and washing basins are typically Victorian as are richly-coloured tapestry bags.

Furniture
This is usually made of dark polished wood, preferably mahogany, although light wood furniture can be stained in imitation. Look for reproduction pieces and second-hand shop finds. Chairs and sofas are often button-backed and deeply upholstered.

Window treatments
Curtains should be heavily draped, in flowered chintz for bedrooms and tasselled velvet for living rooms. Curtains are held back with matching tie-backs during the day, and undercurtains are made of lace.

Soft furnishings
More often than not these are decoratively patterned, although plain fabric is frequently used for upholstery and cushions – velvet and velour are popular choices and Dralon is a good modern alternative.

Floors
Boards are usually stripped and stained or possibly covered with plain carpet. Patterned rugs with an Oriental or Persian feel are then laid on top. Shades of reds, blues and greens are always popular.

Fireplaces
Fireplaces are made of marble or slate in grand rooms and cast iron and painted wood in bedrooms and less important rooms. In Victorian times fires were the main form of heating and cast a soft flickering light which added atmosphere.

▷ **Line and shape**
Furniture is a mixture of the elegant and the heavy. Dark polished woods prevail with plain coloured upholstery. Chairs are balloon back for dining and button back 'Victoria and Albert' for living rooms. Rugs have an Eastern feel.

▽ **Richly patterned**
Fabrics and wallpapers are patterned in regal colours and fresh florals as well. Wallpaper borders can be used at cornice, picture rail and dado height to emphasize or replace architectural details. Curtains, upholstery and tablecloths are trimmed with braids, tassels and lace.

▷ **Accessories**
Choose carved, dark woods for fruit platters, posy holders and trays, patterned china for plant holders and tea sets, brass or china for door handles. Plants should be large with heavy green leaves or fine and feathery.

▽ **Soft and light**
Cushions are fat, fringed and frilled. They feature tapestry designs, patterned chintz, or plain velvet. Reproduction oil lamps and gas wall brackets are more in keeping than central pendants – however, if pendants are used they should be ornate with two or more shades on brass or gilt stems. Pictures depicting rural scenes and botanical prints are typical of the era.

The Edwardian Period

From the 1880s onwards there was a reaction against the heavy, dark and over-furnished interiors of the previous decades. Younger Victorians – the Edwardians – started to favour a simpler, lighter look for their homes. Paler woods such as oak, walnut, birch or sycamore were popular. Paintwork, too, was lighter – cream or white, green, pink or pale yellow.

A key influence on Edwardian design was William Morris, whose Arts and Crafts movement inspired a revolt against the mass-produced machine-made furniture of the earlier Victorian era. Everything from furniture to ceramics was produced by hand and so had a more individual quality.

Other influences were Ambrose Heal, whose pioneering furniture designs favoured a simple construction that allowed the natural beauty of the wood to show, and Liberty, whose famous Art Nouveau prints became one of the most distinctive hallmarks of this period.

Furniture featured curving lines and rounded fronts. Distinctive details include slim, high verticals on chairs and bedheads; hollow hand-holes on drawers instead of metal handles; and plenty of decorative carving on wood.

Wallpaper and fabric designs were inspired by the country and the garden. Roses rambled everywhere, while stylized elongated tulips and irises echoed the lines of the furniture.

Floors were still mostly stained wooden boards with Oriental or Persian-look rugs. Hallways were often tiled, either in chequerboard black and white patterns, or in blues, browns and beiges for more complex designs. In many Edwardian houses tiling beginning on the path outside and continuing along the hallway inside can still be seen. Stained glass provided pattern for the front of the house, and windows and glass doors.

Accessories Plates, bowls and vases were made from embossed pewter or copper. Decorative enamels and new, experimental glazes on pottery provided a wealth of detail and interest.

Bathroom – mellow comfort
Edwardian bathrooms were often full of books, plants, pictures – even chairs. This modern copy features an etched glass screen, brass fittings and mahogany fittings for a true period air.

△ **Dining room – clever mix**
This attractive room emulates a typical
Edwardian mix of shapes and styles,
with dark wood cabinets and airier,
mock-bamboo, rush-seated chairs.

Interesting details are the loop-over
curtain heading and the use of a
papered interior to lighten the dark
wood china cabinet. The rise-and-fall
lamp is also very much of the period.

◁ **Edwardian elegance**
The wooden back of this delicate sofa is
carved in elongated lines (including a
couple of hearts) until there is more air
than wood. Creamy wallpaper covered
in pink roses and lacy cushions add a
feminine touch.

◁ *Sitting room – authentic feel*
This is a good example of how antique and reproduction elements can work together to create an authentic atmosphere. Fabric and wallpaper are adapted from an original William Morris design and all the woods – from the fireplace surround to accessories – are picked for their soft, mellow tones.

▽ *Bathroom – a lighter look*
Light greens were very popular (this was the time when the term 'greenery-yallery' came into vogue). Festooned lace, bracket lights with glass shades, solid, dark wood furniture, and a warm Persian-style rug on the floor are all in keeping with the period mixture of the late Victorian love of mahogany and the Edwardian trend towards a lighter look.

LUXURIANT LIVING

Romantic is undoubtedly the word to describe this pretty, lace-filled bedroom. The Edwardians loved the light, delicate look of lace and used it for everything from window panels to tablecloths, as well as to trim bed linen and covers, cushions and lampshades.

Whereas in downstairs rooms practicality – and a lack of modern cleaning methods – called for heavier and darker fabrics, bedrooms and bathrooms lent themselves to a more self-indulgent approach, inviting pleasure-lovers to relax in easy comfort.

Simpler lines for furniture and lighter floral designs in fabrics gave the Edwardian home an altogether airier, less cluttered feel than its immediate Victorian predecessor. Dark wood furniture was backed by paler walls.

Walls

The overall look is less cluttered than the Victorian mixture of patterns with dozens of pictures. Walls can be papered or painted with the possible addition of a dado rail. Downstairs colours are richer – moss, rust and creamy-beige. Upstairs, pinks, pale greens and white predominate. Patterns are mainly derived from nature with flower or leaf designs.

Windows

As a general rule downstairs fabrics are heavier in weight and warmer in colour. Velvets, brocades, or linen unions are used for curtains, with lace panels stretched over the window. These days lace can be used as curtains or made into ruched blinds.

Lighting

Brass wall brackets, rise-and-fall ceiling pendants, table lamps and standard lamps are all in keeping. Shades are glass, with shapes varying from plain coloured conical to wavy-edged designs and elaborate stained and leaded Tiffany-style.

Accessories

Photographs and prints in silver, walnut or birds-eye maple frames; flowered china, often with unusual glazes as part of the pattern; vases and scent bottles with filigree silver overlays; pewter and copper for plates, tankards and decorative pieces; and enamelware.

Furniture

The Victorian legacy is still seen in mahogany and other dark woods, but wood is usually lighter, with oak being the most common. Furniture shapes are less elaborate. Small circular tables covered with floor-length cloths are still popular for bedrooms and carved wooden bedheads replace cast-iron frames.

Floors

Generally, stained wooden board covered – almost entirely – by rich rugs. Patterned tile floors feature largely in halls, kitchens and bathrooms. Fitted carpets are a more comfortable modern alternative, but add Eastern-style rugs for an authentic feel.

▷ Line and shape

Furniture features simple flowing lines and straight, square legs with minimal detailing. Darker woods become simpler in line. More light woods such as oak, birch and sycamore begin to appear. Upholstery becomes less stuffed and buttoned, more slim and elegant.

Distinctive details are elongated uprights on chairs, extending above curved crest rails, and cut-out motifs, such as hearts on chair backs and cabinet fronts.

◁ Authentic fittings

Shades for pendant lights, table lamps and wall lights are often glass, either etched, stained or left plain. Light fittings sometimes echo stylized floral shapes. Painted wooden dado rails are an important feature and brass figures largely for light fitments and door furniture.

△ Accessories

Flower symbols appear in all sizes and colours. Elongated shapes for items such as candlesticks and cutlery echo the lines of furniture. Lace is everywhere from curtains to table linen.

▷ Colour and pattern

Green, cream and rich red or golds are popular colours for tiles, fabrics and wallcoverings. Rich floral patterns are balanced with plain colours. Dado rails divide plain walls and embossed designs, such as this original Edwardian one in Lincrusta, are still available. Fringing and tassels add interest to plain fabrics, but only in moderation.

A Feel for the Thirties

Suburban homes were the first to feel the full force of 1930s streamlined car, boat and train design. Living rooms and bedrooms were filled with large, rounded ocean liner-style furniture in blond woods trimmed with chrome.

But perhaps the most famous 30s design influence was Art Deco. The name derives from the 1925 Paris exhibition of Decorative and Industrial Arts where exhibits had to represent contemporary lifestyles. Out went the flowing lines and muted pastel colours of Art Nouveau. In came bright oranges, mauves, lime greens and angular lines inspired by the contemporary *Ballet Russe* sets and costumes. Other design influences owed more to the discovery of Tutankhamun's tomb: Egyptian ornament was popular. The stepped 'ziggurat' terraces of Aztec temples were also to be seen everywhere.

Walls were marbled or ragged in cream and beige while simple friezes were much in evidence. Floorcoverings were good-quality parquet, linoleum and rugs. Improved plywood moulding techniques also affected furniture design and shape, with rounded corners an important feature. Chrome, glass, leather and black lacquer were popular combined with pale sycamore, bird's eye maple, walnut and light oak and other, dark woods.

Windows had wooden pelmets, painted or covered with fabric with jagged motifs picked out in paint or tape. Venetian blinds in metal or wood were alternatives to curtains. Typical light fittings were opal glass bowl lamps, bronze and chrome lady bases.

Dining area – black and chrome
A modern sophisticated interpretation of 1930s style, with black-stained oak furniture and a pale grey, apricot and tan colour scheme.

△ Living room – tiled fireplace
Ceramic 30s-look tiles and ornaments make a focal point of this decorative fireplace. The fireplace opening has been filled in with a board covered in mirror tiles.

△ Classic trolley
This chrome and glass trolley has 30s Hollywood appeal yet still fits in well with modern interiors. It is one of the many copies of original 1930s designs which are still widely available.

▷ Bedroom – liner looks
Luxury looks redolent of the Queen Mary are seen with these built-in bedside fittings of blond and black wood combined with generous panels of mirror. Scalloped edging on the bed linen softens the severe streamlined look of the bed and its built-in sofa. Strip lamps concealed behind coving mouldings provide softly-diffused atmospheric background lighting.

◁ Bedroom – decorative
An original maple bedroom suite with the typically rounded corners seen on furniture of the period. Accessories are an important part of creating the 30s mood. Face wall plaques and vases are still readily found in antique markets and large circular mirrors are available in DIY outlets.

BRIGHT IDEA

ADDING A MOTIF

Stepped Aztec-inspired 'ziggurat' designs and Egyptian sunrise motifs were seen everywhere during the 1930s and were used to decorate furniture and windows.

You can apply an Art Deco-style motif to plain flush-fronted modern storage units using self-adhesive rigid plastic edging strip. The strip is available from larger DIY shops and is approximately 12mm wide; it comes in a wide range of colours, including pastel shades and bright primaries. Use a sharp trimming knife or sharp household scissors to cut the strips and arrange them into different shapes to decorate a plain surface.

Arranging storage units to create a stepped outline also helps to emphasize the 30s feeling to great effect.

PUTTING ON THE RITZ

Take from the style as much or as little as you like: a rounded, chrome and glass occasional table or rugs with geometric motifs, perhaps. Choose venetian blinds or curtains in Art Deco geometric prints and match up motifs with a stencilled border on sponged walls. Pick seating with smooth, curved backs and sides with fat rectangular cushions. Show

wood can be of lacquered wood, pale ash or light oak. Upholstery can be leather or figured moquette in soft orangey golds or pinks and greys.

Art Deco sunrise and geometric rug patterns have recently been reproduced to fit in with modern colour schemes. These blend happily with some genuine period pieces. There are still real bargains to be had in 1930s

dining furniture, sideboards, wardrobes and dressing tables. Painted cream or black they can look very modern. Look out for Art Deco pottery vases and jugs in primary colours and fill them with fake blooms. Decorative cut-glass dressing table sets in pastel colours and items of *pate de verre* (opaque) glass, bakelite plastic clocks, mirrors and photo frames are inexpensive.

Accessories
Statuettes, particularly female figures; pottery decorated in bright orange, yellow and green geometric and stylized flower designs. Have a set of cocktail glasses and a chrome shaker.

Lighting
The overall effect is soft and atmospheric. A marbled glass bowl pendant hanging on chains, stylized figure table lamp, wall and freestanding uplighters are all typical of the 1930s.

Walls
Plain painted, sponged, stippled or papered with an all-over geometric or stylized floral print. Creams and beige were favourite colours. Borders were used at picture rail or ceiling height and also to divide a wall into framed panels.

Furniture
Look out for sideboards, dressing tables, wardrobes, dining tables and chairs with rounded corners and in pale woods and exotic veneers such as bird's eye maple, sycamore, walnut and light oak. Chrome and glass tables and trolleys are useful extras.

Seating
Thirties upholstery was made to last; leather was popular but more usually, three-pieces suites were covered in moquette – either cut to give a velvety pile or uncut, to give a looped effect. Seating frames were often of bent plywood or chrome.

Flooring
Lino in beige, brown, creams and green was popular in hallways, kitchens and bathrooms. Polished parquet or woodblock floors with rugs featuring geometric motifs were used in living rooms.

Stencilled motifs
A geometric 30s-style stencil creates a more modern effect by combining it with a simple painted stripe running along the top of the wall and about a third of the way down at each corner.

▷ *Essential lighting*
Appropriate lighting is a vital ingredient when re-creating the 30s style. This selection of reproduction fittings is representative of the period and can all be purchased at various specialist lighting shops.

▽ *Line and shape*
Sleek, streamlined forms and geometric shapes as reflected in a 'ziggurat'-top mirror, set the scene. The curve of the sides of the chair is broken by the square shape of the seat. The curve is repeated on the sunrise-shaped lamp and horseshoe-foot table.

△ **Accessories**
Authentic objects from the 1930s give the finishing touches if you want to achieve this look. Fortunately, bric-a-brac, clocks, pottery and glass can still be found inexpensively on market stalls and in junk shops.

▽ **Fabrics and paper**
Add a wallpaper border with a geometric motif to a plain wall. Look for shagreen (imitation sharkskin) papers and fabrics and figured chenille upholstery fabrics.

The Best of Italy

Necessity is the mother of invention and nowhere is this more apparent perhaps than in Italy, where most people live in small flats and designers enjoy a reputation for being masters of space saving, dual-purpose furniture.

Tables, for instance, may open envelope-fashion or have an ingenious single flap on one side to turn a console into a dining table. Deceptively simple wall storage units can house all the household clutter with sections that pull out to make tables or desks.

Modern Italian seating relies very much on clean-cut, definite lines. The conventional three-piece suite has no place here. Instead, individual chairs are used to make design statements. A simple upholstered sofa can be contrasted with a chair of shiny chrome, wire-mesh or plastic.

And rather than using conventional fixed upholstery which cannot be easily cleaned, upholstery can be closely 'wrapped' with practical, removable fabric covers. Other seating may have functional metal frames with tailoring details, such as flat cushions to replace upholstered arms and a top section which opens out to form a high back or folds down to make a neck support.

Lighting is important. Freestanding uplighters and multi-adjustable angular desk lights in chrome and matt black metal frequently punctuate living rooms, bedrooms and work rooms. Pendant lights favour space-age shapes and hang low over coffee or dining tables.

Hallway – light and airy
White walls and a painted floor provide a neutral background to this sculptural table. The lilies echo the arrangement of canes in the umbrella stand; a geometric patterned rug echoes the colours of the painting above.

▷ **Living room – flexible seating**
Piero de Martini designed this sculptural seating range called 'Sampan'. It comprises individual, horseshoe-shaped chairs which can be covered in a choice of traditional floral or plain fabrics. Units can be used singly or very simply linked together to form a variety of seating arrangements.

▽ **Dining area – space-saving table**
A simple shelving unit transforms into a neat envelope-flap-shaped table for two. The striking black, white and yellow colour scheme is echoed in the shelving, black and yellow chairs and tiled floor.

△ **Living room – practical comfort**
These 'Cardigan' sofas were designed by Vico Magistretti, one of Italy's foremost designers and have the look of almost being 'wrapped up' in padded fabric covers that unzip for cleaning. The 'Veranda' chair in the background has adjustable head support and foot rest.

▷ **Kitchen – functional design**
Shiny laminate, built-in appliances and lots of cleanly-tiled surfaces make up this modern streamlined kitchen. The small grid created by the wall tiles is picked up on a larger scale on the floor. The almost all-white scheme is accented by touches of black in the taps, venetian blinds and bar stools.

COLOUR AND PATTERN

Colour schemes are definite: either clear pastels, brilliant primaries, or black and white. Upholstery fabrics are usually in plain colours in flat or self-patterned weaves, stripes, checks or small geometric patterns. Some animal prints such as zebra stripes or leopard prints are also included. Flowers are not usually incorporated as part of this look – and if flowery fabrics are used, it is to complement a particular shape of furniture or to make a one-off design statement.

A chair may have a plain black back, a blue seat and maybe yellow arms; other seating in the room then tends to be in plain colours, perhaps with black used for occasional tables. A sofa in navy and cream check may be offset by a seating unit incorporating a chaise longue section in a clear red.

Glossy lacquers in black, cream, grey and red are often used for tables and storage. Natural or stained black ash is popular for chair frames as well as tubular black metal and chrome.

Windows mostly feature blinds – either venetian, plain roller, or pinoleum. Curtains, if used, tend to be plain with tailored triple-pleat or pencil headings, hung from track rather than poles. Floors are of highly polished wood – or, alternatively, ceramic or vinyl tiles, painted wood or marble. Good quality art rugs with geometric patterns are a more suitable choice for this look than fitted carpet.

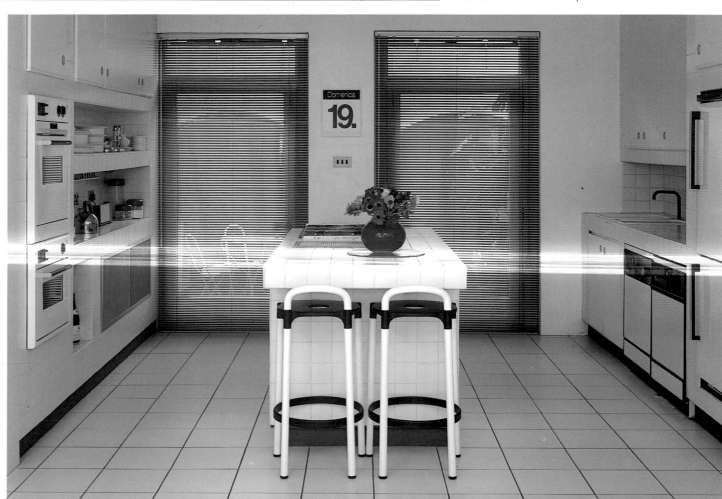

ACHIEVING THE LOOK

Italian furniture is often very expensive, so aim to make an impact with one or two good examples with elegant simple lines – a single chair and light fitting perhaps. Look for old sofas and occasional chairs that can be re-covered in plain upholstery fabrics in primary colours. Coffee tables shaped like an artist's palette, with splayed metal legs can be given a coat of black gloss paint for a modern Italian look.

Window treatments can be plain roller or venetian blinds. Floors should be plain with a hard surface; parquet or vinyl marble-look floor tiles from DIY shops are an inexpensive answer. Add interest with geometric patterned rugs. Walls should be painted plain white or cream for displaying traditional and modern abstract paintings.

Walls
Ceramics in plain neutral colours are mostly used for kitchen and bathroom walls. Other surfaces are painted white or cream to display traditional and modern paintings, posters and prints.

Lighting
Functional, adjustable lights with clean, dramatic lines are an integral part of this look. Choose tall, floor-standing uplighters; hang pendants low over dining tables and to define seating areas. Pick flexible task lights for bedrooms and living rooms.

Windows
Shutters or plain blinds in understated colours – beige, cream, white and grey – are best suited to this look.

Flooring
Polished or painted wood, ceramic or vinyl tiles in plain colours or with the look of marble or stone, set off this cool modern style. Add a rug in a geometric pattern for warmth and to complement the colours and shapes in the room.

Accessories
Keep these to a minimum. Choose only pieces which are functional or have a real contribution to make to the scheme: large vases which pick up an accent colour or add impact with their shape. A piece of sculpture could make a secondary focal point.

Furniture
Beds are streamlined in shape, tables and shelves are built into recesses beside the bed or as part of a headboard. The cantilevered chair is typically Italian in style.

▽ **Accessories**
Choose objects which are functional,
echo a line which appears elsewhere or
make an additional focal point in a room
– plain glass containers for flowers,
marbles or shells, a vase for colour or
pattern accent, perhaps a piece of
sculpture.

▷ **Essentials**
Lighting is nearly as important as
furniture in creating the Italian look.
Leggy uplighters, versatile work lights
and stylish pendants are almost pieces
of sculpture in their own right, as well as
being efficient light sources.

△ Line and shape

Shapes are mainly streamlined, with wrapped and folded 'tailoring' details to add interest. Witty and practical pieces – chairs and occasional tables – are used for impact. This 'T-line' chair has a padded back which extends to the floor with dramatically cantilevered seat. The lacquered coffee table owes as much impact to its boldly-sweeping curves as to its high gloss and bright colour. A multi-position 'Dove' light appears poised for flight.

▽ Surfaces

Wood or vinyl tiles which simulate marble or stone are a good choice for floors. Upholstery fabrics in plain colours or geometric patterns are usual; often fabrics have surface interest – self-patterned weaves, repps, pile or subtly-quilted materials.

Classic Blond Scandinavian

This Scandinavian style fits well into urban environments, despite its emphasis on wood and natural fibres. Clean lines and practical, built-in furniture coupled with freshly-coloured abstract-design fabrics add up to a look that is at once contemporary yet easy.

The Finnish architect Alvar Aalto provided the inspiration for this look in the 1930s, when he initiated the technique of steaming and shaping layers of wood for his furniture. Using birch, he made the most of the natural spring of the material to produce sweeping curves, supported by bentwood frames. His original styles are still produced today and have a timeless quality well suited to modern interiors.

It is not, however, necessary to have this original furniture to create the look. Light woods on a background of neutral tones, enlivened with bright splashes of colour, and flowing lines rather than sharp edges can achieve the same result.

Plenty of wood is essential, though, for furniture and floors and, if possible, for walls and ceilings too. Crafted items such as nubbly rugs and loose-weave fabrics also help to create the look.

IMPORTANCE OF TEXTURE

Textured textiles to contrast with the smooth wood finish is another important feature of this look. And in keeping with the use of natural wood, natural fibres are favoured as much as possible.

Large expanses of wood flooring need something to break them up, so main areas are covered with large tufted or woven wool rugs, often in neutral tones, while brightly-coloured cotton rugs are scattered elsewhere.

Living area – classic look

Classic Scandinavian furniture is grouped on a large tufted rug and colour is minimal in this typical living area. Wood is used for both ceiling and floor and the curtains are pulled well back to make the most of available light.

LIGHTING AND COLOUR

Plain, simply-decorated rooms lacking any period detail suit this style best, with generous windows that allow plenty of light to enter. Window treatments should be kept simple – either roller or roman blinds or floor-length curtains with simple pencil-pleat headings. They should have enough space at the side so that they can be drawn clear of the frame.

Artificial lighting is as streamlined as possible. Recessed light fittings are ideal, but free-standing lamps with simply-styled lampshades present a practical alternative to lowering a ceiling in order to install concealed lighting.

Colours are clear, and sharply-defined against the background of natural wood. Shades of pink and blue complement wood better than hot oranges or yellow.

Accessories should add to the easy-living feel of this style. Glassware and ceramics with simple, clean lines are ideal – as are small ornaments and functional accessories in plain wood. Plenty of indoor plants also help to take away any clinical air engendered by this practical, easy-to-clean style.

△ *Sitting room – simple*
In this small sitting room the Scandinavian look has been achieved at relatively little cost but to great effect. A simple cane blind echoes the natural look of the wicker chair and wood floor, while gaily-checked fabrics and a bright rug liven up the whole room.

◁ *Child's room – bright*
Here the style provides inspiration for decorating a child's room. Large built-in cupboards and sparse furniture add up to a room which is uncluttered and easy to keep clean and tidy. Brightly-coloured fabrics in bold patterns contrast with the simple functional furniture.

◁ *Study – softly green*
This study room has an easy, fresh appeal which, combined with the light wood furniture and wall storage units, is very Scandinavian in style. The sheer blinds take away the glare but still allow plenty of soft diffused light to enter. Elegant modern uplighters throw a gentle light on to the ceiling when background lighting is needed.

▽ *Work area – stylish*
A classic cantilevered chair is teamed up with this sleek wall unit to make an updated version of the original 1930s Scandinavian style. A stylish desk lamp that serves as task lighting and the elegant ornaments in the display cabinet are typically Scandinavian.

◁ *Bathroom – clean and practical*
Eminently practical, this Scandinavian style is ideally suited to bathrooms. Here the clean lines of the white tiling are saved from being clinical by the splashes of bright red accents and blond wood trimmings and ceiling. As well as visually warming up the room, the wood lends a 'sauna' look which is thoroughly in keeping with the style. A lively rag rug would make a perfect bath mat.

ELEMENTS OF STYLE

This bedroom is typical of Scandinavian style. Well-made and practical, the furniture is designed to look good in any modern setting. You don't have to use birchwood – used to perfection in the classic Alvar Aalto designs of the 30s; instead look for any light wood furniture that reproduces the style's clean, simple lines. Inexpensive pieces are often quite easy to find.

The look's tendency to clinical simplicity can be offset by using natural materials – wood in abundance, cotton, wool or linen in fabrics and rugs. Add splashes of colour – at the window or on the floor, or in simple light fittings.

As this style is predominantly functional, accessories are not that relevant, just enough items of everyday use to provide a lived-in feeling. Leafy houseplants are used throughout the house, perhaps to bring interest to the long and bitter Scandinavian winter.

Lighting
Essentially functional, recessed fittings are first choice for general overhead lighting. For task lighting choose modern streamlined designs for pendant, standard and table lamps.

Windows
Window treatments are simple. Use plain roman blinds to complement your colour scheme, rattan roller blinds, or curtains with plain pencil-pleat headings that reach the floor. Fabrics are either neutral weaves or brightly-coloured cottons with large overall designs.

Walls
Make the most of natural light by using clear fresh colours or plain white emulsion; pale blue is a good choice to offset the warmth of wood.

Furniture
As much fitted furniture as possible in birch and other light woods. Closed wall cupboards to provide ample storage space. Smooth, flowing lines with rounded edges and no sharp corners on both fitted and free-standing furniture.

Flooring
Fitted neutral carpet is often the choice for bedrooms. Living areas tend to be more practical – easy-to-clean wood brightened up with highly-coloured rugs.

Accessories
Smoothly-styled glassware, chrome or ceramics that have a functional purpose as well. Plenty of house plants and a small amount of lived-in clutter provide an unpretentious atmosphere.

Tudor and Jacobean Styles

Many people own a real or reproduction piece of antique furniture. For the novice it is notoriously difficult to tell the difference between a real antique and a reproduction, or even between different historical styles, so it can help to know a little about the changing fashions in furniture through our history.

During the 16th and 17th centuries, England's growing prosperity was reflected in the demand for a wider variety of furniture to fill the many new houses which were being built.

The florid version of renaissance style which was coming in to England from Germany and the Netherlands suited ostentatious Elizabethan taste. Furniture was ornate and it was unusual to find a piece of furniture without some kind of decoration. Elaborate inlay work, interlacing scrolls, strap-like bands and formal flower patterns covered the surfaces, while legs were carved into bulbous forms.

The commonest wood was oak, sometimes inlaid with other woods. Surviving oak furniture has darkened naturally with age, unlike the Tudor-style furniture of the 19th and 20th centuries which was dark-stained or varnished.

Along with the increasing prosperity came a growing desire for comfort. Chairs were lighter, easily moved, and many more of them were comfortably upholstered in velvet or silk.

Jacobean furniture mostly followed Elizabethan forms but was a little less florid. The completely upholstered bed, fashionable on the continent, became popular in England's great houses, with matching chairs and stools upholstered in the same fabrics.

RESTORATION TO QUEEN ANNE

The puritan dislike for anything elaborate kept furniture simple and basic during the Commonwealth but with the restoration of the monarchy, a reaction set in. Charles II had continental ideas of comfort and a taste for the Baroque style.

Both furniture and houses were destroyed in the Great Fire of London in 1666 and the roomier, lighter houses with painted pine panelling and delicately-moulded plaster ceilings that replaced them called for lighter, more elegant furniture. Walnut replaced oak and veneering became popular. Veneering made it possible to use beautifully-marked woods that were small in section or fragile. A variety of coloured woods, even ebony, mother of pearl and ivory were cut, like the pieces of a jigsaw puzzle, to build up pictorial designs (called marquetry) or geometric patterns of contrasting woods (called parquetry).

Lacquering also became fashionable, and many lacquered chests and panels were imported from the Orient.

It was Indian furniture that first introduced cane to Europe. Cane mesh was used for chair and couch seats as well as chair backs, making them lighter, more comfortable and cheaper. Cane contrasted well with the flamboyant, elaborate carving typical of the Restoration chair.

Furniture became leaner and taller throughout the William and Mary period. Decoration grew more restrained.

By the end of the 17th century, the life of the English gentleman had become more relaxed and this is reflected in the less elaborate furniture of Queen Anne's reign – beauty of line was preferred to ornament. The S-shaped curve was the most important element of this furniture. Marquetry and parquetry were discarded in favour of all-over veneers, usually of walnut. Textiles for upholstery and hangings were the major source of decoration and a high standard of embroidery resulted.

COURT CUPBOARD/BUFFET OF OAK
Style Unique to England and designed to hold the family silver. It consists of two or three open shelves with drawers in the friezes. The supports are bulbous in form or are carved into grotesque beasts.

ELIZABETHAN POSTER BED
Style Heavily-carved tester supported in front by two freestanding posts with 'cup and cover' decoration. Supported at the head by a carved and inlaid headboard. Tudor and Jacobean beds were prestige pieces and highly prized.

PANEL-BACKED CHAIR
Style A light and comfortable style of chair. The boxed-in base of earlier styles has gone, and the back is angled for comfort. It is also carved and inlaid.

OAK DRAW-LEAF REFECTORY TABLE

Style A new piece which was useful in the comparatively small dining room – it is still popular today for that reason. The top rests unattached on a frame supported by heavy legs linked by stretchers. Two leaves resting under the main table can be pulled out.

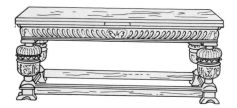

KNOLE SOFA

Style One of the earliest styles of upholstered sofa. The hinged, padded headrests which are attached to each arm can be adjusted to form a day bed. This style is still made today.

OVAL GATE-LEG TABLE (c1680)

Style A space-saving piece of furniture for seating up to 12 people. It has a handy cutlery/napery drawer. Small versions are still useful and popular for small dining rooms.

UPHOLSTERED BED (Late 17th century)

Style Wooden bed base with an elaborately upholstered bedhead and tester. Bed-posts of great height are completely hidden by drapery.

JAMES II CHEST OF DRAWERS (c1685)

Style The chests used for storage in the 16th and 17th centuries had no internal divisions so that boxes had to be used inside for storing goods. Doors were put in front for easy access and so gradually the chest of drawers evolved. This one has oyster-walnut and marquetry veneers.

IMPORTED LACQUERED CABINET (c1680)

Style Cabinets arrived from the East without stands. As they were highly prized, expensive pieces, elaborately carved gilt or silvered stands were made to support them. These cabinets were made with various wood bases and covered with as many as 15 coats of lacquer.

CHARLES II CANE ARMCHAIR

Style Split cane seat and back panel with barley-sugar twist uprights. It has a carved cresting rail and a front stretcher with the 'boyes and crown' device of the Restoration period. The bold carving is of flowers and foliage.

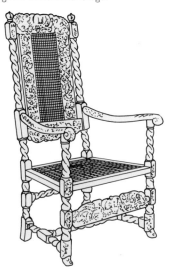

HOOPED-BACK DINING CHAIR (c1715)

Style The solid splat back on this walnut chair is curved to fit the occupant's spine. The chair has a wide, drop-in upholstered seat. There is a curved front rail and graceful cabriole legs with claw and ball feet and restrained carvings.

QUEEN ANNE KNEE-HOLE DESK (c1710)

Style The drawers surround a hinged cupboard compartment. Usually made in walnut with brass handles and lock. Has good storage space and is also useful as a small dressing table.

TALLBOY OR CHEST-ON-CHEST

Style A distinctive piece with bracket feet and fluted canted corners. Some versions had a pull-out tray dividing the sets of drawers.

Georgian Styles of Furniture

During the early Georgian period furniture developed along two distinctive lines. The domestic style of Queen Anne continued with minor changes in design – notably more elaborate carving – until mid-century. Imported mahogany grew in popularity and replaced French walnut which became scarce in the 1720s. Not only does mahogany have a beautiful variety of figuring and colouring, its hardness makes it ideal for detailed carving and it yields wide boards suitable for wardrobes and tables.

The second trend in furniture design was strongly Italianate in manner. It is particularly associated with William Kent, a multi-talented architect, interior decorator and furniture designer. Through his involvement in building, decorating and furnishing houses, he produced the first fully-integrated interiors in Britain.

Only the grandest furniture could stand up to his opulent interiors and, like its Italian prototypes, his furniture was monumental rather than comfortable. His chairs became thrones and his beds dominant architectural features. Kent's ideas were adapted by other craftsmen making less flamboyant and more comfortable furniture for the great houses of the 1730s and 1740s.

ROCOCO INFLUENCES

It was mid-century before the extravagant ornament typical of the Rococo style, so loved on the continent, began to appear in fashionable English houses.

Many richly-coloured woods became popular for their decorative properties. Ornament was employed lavishly – almost every surface was embellished with painted, carved, woven, modelled, cast and embossed decorations. Pictorial marquetry and geometric parquetry were favoured, as well as paintings of idyllic pastoral scenes using new coloured varnishes.

Some cabinet makers imitated imported Chinese furniture but these adaptations bore little likeness to the originals. However, they did enrich British design with new features – rich lacquering, lattice work patterns on chair backs, miniature Chinese railings edging small tables, pagoda roofs on beds and so on.

Another fashionable frivolity was the revival of 'Gothic' styles. Although these bore little resemblance to true medieval designs. Gothic motifs such as pointed arches, fleurs de lys and quatrefoils were freely applied to all types of furniture. Not surprisingly for a period typically frivolous rather than purist. Gothic and Chinese were sometimes combined in the same piece!

THOMAS CHIPPENDALE (1718–79)

All these fanciful motifs were incorporated in the repertoire of Chippendale, the most renowned English furniture maker. His influential book of designs – The Gentleman and Cabinet-Maker's Director, published in 1754 – was intended as a guide to customers as well as a pattern book for tradesmen, and helped spread his ideas widely.

Chippendale produced some of the most comfortable chairs of the 18th century – typically with broad, upholstered seats and backs. A squarer look replaced the curves of the early years of the century, cabriole legs gave way to square legs chamfered on the inside, and the centre splat was pierced, often with elaborate carving of Rococo, Gothic, Chinese or ribbon motifs.

ROBERT ADAM (1728–92)

Adam developed his own style of furniture to suit the simpler, clearer lines of his classically-inspired interiors. Chair legs, for example, became more elegant and lighter – slender, straight supports tapered to the foot. Wall furniture dominated his work – pier tables surmounted by delicate tripartite mirrors, girandoles and commodes. Urns on pedestals flanked side tables and the modern sideboard developed from this ensemble.

SHERATON & HEPPLEWHITE

No single piece of furniture has been authenticated as having been made by either Sheraton or Hepplewhite yet their names are used to categorize two styles of later Georgian design. Oval, hoop, heart-shaped and particularly shield-shaped chair backs are typical of Hepplewhite's style, along with the Prince of Wales' feather motif. His light beech chairs, lacquered or painted, with cane seats were popular.

The arts of veneering, inlay and marquetry reached great heights at this time. There was a fondness for lighter coloured woods, often with painted decoration by well-known artists or with inset ceramic panels.

As the 18th century progressed, fashionable taste veered towards greater simplicity of line and decoration, exemplified by the work of the cabinet-maker Thomas Sheraton. He made little use of Adam's decorative motifs but used contrasting veneers laid in oval or lozenge-shaped patterns set off by black or brass stringing lines and borders of cross-banding. He re-introduced delicate, square and rectangular forms for mirrors, chair backs and sofas. Chair backs were lower than previously and the arms swept strongly upwards to meet the back at the cresting rail. The simple construction of many of his designs made them cheap and easy for country craftsmen to reproduce.

THE REGENCY PERIOD

Regency style takes its name from the Prince of Wales who was Prince Regent 1811–20. The lack of living space in the new town houses of the period encouraged the design of ingenious space-saving, dual-purpose furniture.

In addition to earlier interest in ancient Rome together with Chinese and Gothic influences, classical Greece became a dominant influence and a new interest in Egypt was aroused in the years following Nelson's triumph at the Battle of the Nile in 1798.

Pieces of furniture were actually copied from vase paintings which were being excavated in ever increasing quantities. Thus versions of the Greek 'Klismos' chair appeared and the Grecian sofa was a characteristic Regency piece. Its companion, the new sofa table, also made an appearance.

Wood inlay was too expensive for many people and carving was a dying art. Thus favourites were dark and glossy mahogany and rosewood and highly grained species such as amboyna and zebra wood. Brass, which was cheap, durable and looked well against dark woods, became the main decorative feature in the form of thin stringing lines, inlays of sheet brass cut into floral or scroll forms and, for expensive pieces, elaborate inlay. Brass galleries around sideboards, wire trellis work on cabinet doors, and brass castors for chairs and tables were common.

GEORGE I BUREAU CABINET
Style In burr walnut and with an elaborately fitted interior with secret compartments. Follows the tradition established during the reign of Queen Anne.

GEORGE II TEA TABLE
Style A portable mahogany table with simple pie-crust decoration around the top and a carved tripod base. The hinged top folds over for easy storage – and allowed the table to double as a firescreen. The fashion for taking tea or coffee after dinner made such pieces of furniture popular, and it remained in favour throughout the 18th and 19th centuries. Variations were made for use as wine, supper or breakfast tables. ·

STATE BED BY WILLIAM KENT (1732)
Style One hundred yards of velvet went into this enormous upholstered bed. The bedhead, itself upholstered, is surmounted by a great double shell with spines picked out in braid. The architectural character of the canopy is emphasized by gold braiding.

SIDE-TABLE BY KENT
Style A great slab of marble is supported by an extravagantly carved and gilded base – crouching sphinxes and festoons of foliage are attached to scrolled legs. Such side-tables, usually surmounted by mirrors, were designed to fit in with the architectural character of rooms.

ROCOCO GIRANDOLE (1758)
Style This girandole – an Italian term for an ornate wall light, often with both a mirror and candles – represents one of the more bizarre expressions of English Rococo. Swirling branches support a weird collection of creatures.

STYLES AND PERIODS
Tudor/Jacobean covers the reigns of Henry VIII, Elizabeth I, James I, Charles I, the Commonwealth period under Cromwell and the Restoration of Charles II (1660).
Queen Anne (reigned 1702–14) stylistically covers a wide period, about 1690 to 1720s.
Georgian is a loose term as there were four Georges who reigned between 1714 and 1830, including the Regency (1811–20). In this period came Baroque, Rococo, Gothic, Chinese, Neo-Classical and Empire influences.
Victorian (1839–1901) The early period is very similar to Biedermeier furniture, while mid-Victorian is heavy and over-fussy, often machine-made. The later part of the reign saw the Arts & Crafts movement develop.

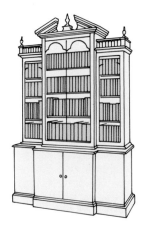

ROCOCO DRESSING TABLE (c1760)
Style An elaborately shaped top supports a mirror embellished with intricately-carved ribbon decoration. This theme is echoed in the swathes of drapery which hide the base and disguise the mirror frame.

MAHOGANY BREAKFRONT BOOKCASE (c1760)
Style The central, projecting section of this substantial bookcase is surmounted by a broken pediment, the side sections have a fretwork gallery. A base of closed cupboards is topped by bookshelves with glazed doors.

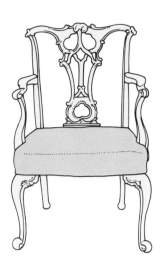

CHIPPENDALE OPEN ARMCHAIR (1760)
Style This typical piece has slender cabriole legs, a generous seat for full skirts, shaped arms to offer comfortable support and an open curved splat in the Gothic manner.

THREE-TIER DUMB WAITER (Mid 18th century)
Style This table afforded diners greater privacy by enabling them to dispense with the services of a waiter. The arched tripod base is decorated with acanthus leaf carvings.

CHIPPENDALE 'CHINESE' CHAIR (c1760)
Style Mahogany chinoiserie chair with a pierced splat back and cluster column legs.

MAHOGANY FRETWORK SECRETAIRE
Style A delicate space-saving writing desk with a hinged front that drops down to provide a writing surface. Many types of secretaire were made between the 16th and 19th centuries. This example has a chinoiserie fretwork gallery.

ROBERT ADAM PIER TABLE (c1772)
Style Designed to stand against a wall, this table is surmounted by an elaborate tripartite mirror with classical decoration and flanked by tripods in the classical manner holding candelabra.

HEPPLEWHITE COVEBACK BERGÈRE CHAIR
Style A comfortable mahogany armchair with a high, curved back and a relatively wide, deep seat. Bergère chairs were generally fully upholstered, and there was usually a deep loose cushion in the seat for extra comfort. The style is simple and the carving is restrained.

SATINWOOD AND MARQUETRY COMMODE
Style Commodes – low pieces of furniture with drawers and sometimes cupboards as well – were used in drawing rooms. This example boasts oval, Adam-style painted panels of classical subjects.

SHIELD-BACK CHAIR (c1785)
Style Designed in the manner of George Hepplewhite, this chair has simple, uncluttered lines. The legs are square in section and taper towards the base; the arms meet the back halfway up the shield and the central splat is carved with Prince of Wales' feathers.

SHERATON SQUARE-BACK CHAIR
Style The arms of this chair sweep upwards to join the back at the cresting rail. The tapering front legs are round in section.

REGENCY CHAISE LONGUE

Style This elegant rosewood chaise longue with inlaid brass decoration would have been used as a day bed.

SHERATON-STYLE SIDEBOARD (c1793)

Style This piece illustrates how the side table combined with pedestals and urns to form the sideboard.

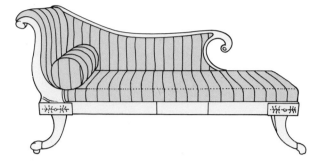

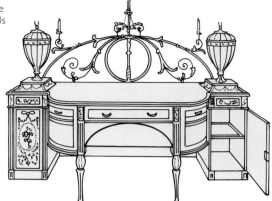

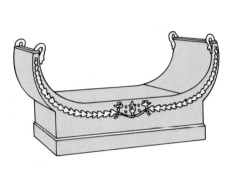

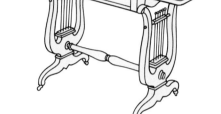

BOAT-SHAPED BED IN EMPIRE STYLE

Style Classical influences are clearly visible. The curving sides, the gilded sprays of berried foliage, and the swan and lyre motifs are favourite decorations of the period.

MAHOGANY SOFA TABLE (c1810)

Style Introduced in the 18th century, the sofa table was usually positioned along the back of the sofa, which was placed centrally in the room.

REGENCY MAHOGANY DRUM TABLE

Style A low table, often leather-topped, with small tapering drawers around the circumference of the circular top. The lockable drawers were used for storing private papers.

DAVENPORT WRITING DESK (c1820)

Style A Davenport is a small desk with a sloping front above drawers. Made of rosewood with a simple pierced rail, this example has a sliding top above a locker, and four drawers which open down one side. There is also a handy pen drawer and pull-out sliders. The Davenport desk is possibly named after a Colonel Davenport who ordered such a desk in the late 18th century. Early examples were simple and elegant – Victorian ones became over elaborate.

CARLTON HOUSE DESK

Style Thought to have been first made for the Prince of Wales in the late 18th century and named after

his London house. A useful collection of small drawers and pigeon holes enclose the sides and back of the desk.

MAHOGANY TRAFALGAR CHAIR

Style Named after the Battle of Trafalgar (1805), the chair has a central motif of anchors and rope turning on the top rail. The scimitar legs are a feature of Regency furniture.

THREE-PART DINING TABLE

Style Large dining tables with removable leaves did not come into general use in this country until the 1780s; before then guests dined at several smaller tables. The forerunner of the modern dining table, it remains useful since the leaves can be stored separately when not needed.

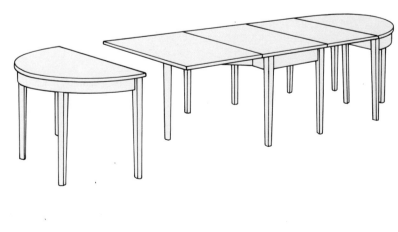

Nineteenth Century Furniture

In the early part of the 19th century, it was still style rather than technology that dominated design. The Biedermeier style of Austria and Germany produced attractive and restrained furniture, with parallels in most countries. This was followed by a swing to romanticism in Europe bringing a rehash of past styles. In Britain the main reproduction styles were Greek, Gothic, Elizabethan (a vague term covering Henry VIII to the Restoration) and Rococo (misnamed Louis XIV).

The so-called 'naturalistic' look which also became popular was an offshoot of the Louis XIV style. Its rich, naturalistic carving, swelling forms and plump upholstery induced a feeling of comfort and well-being.

Whatever the historical basis of early Victorian furniture, it is notable for the rounded forms that are clear in balloon-back chairs, sofas, chiffoniers (a later version of the commode but with many more drawers) and dressing tables.

As the desire for comfort increased, the upholsterer took on a leading role in furniture design and, by the 1830s, dominated seat-making. A patent for coil-spring upholstery was taken out in 1828 and deep-sprung upholstery, often with a deep-buttoned finish, dramatically changed the appearance of seating. On earlier pieces the framework was exposed but it gradually became covered by the upholstery.

Towards the middle of the 19th century, Britain's rapidly-expanding middle classes, with a taste for the better things in life, posed problems and forced change in the furniture trade. Traditional methods of furniture-making were unable to cope with demand and a production line came into use, with each man making just one part of the finished article.

The use of steam-driven machinery enabled furniture to be produced cheaply and quickly. It also turned the exacting task of slicing veneers into a much simpler one, so that veneered furniture became much cheaper and demand increased, though this de-valued it in the eyes of the connoisseur. The introduction of French polish (made from shellac dissolved in spirits) enabled the semi-skilled worker to achieve a shining surface quickly and with little effort. Before this, furniture had to be laboriously polished with beeswax and turpentine or linseed oil to develop a fine patina.

THE REFORM MOVEMENT

The Great Exhibition of 1851 showed that although British manufacturers led the world in technology and the use of new materials, their design was poor. There was a misconception that a little art added to manufactured goods would produce good design – the result was merely an excess of ornament. However, there was a group of reformers already aware of this and they made efforts to change the face of British design.

The writings of the architect Augustus Pugin laid down guidelines for the reformers. He emphasized the need for integrity in design: utility should direct design and ornament should enhance the structure. In his own furniture designs he shunned current methods and turned back to those of medieval joiners. He saw machinery as an aid which should not interfere with the integrity of design. But John Ruskin, a philosopher, believed that the machine could easily degrade man. His ideas, as set out in 'On the nature of Gothic' (1851) became the cornerstone of the Arts and Crafts Movement.

William Morris was the central figure in this group of reformers who finally swung public taste away from over-elaborate ornament. Morris and his pre-Raphaelite friends started designing furniture and fabrics for their own homes and eventually formed the firm of Morris, Marshall and Faulkener. Although Morris aimed to provide beautiful things for the average man, most of his products, which were hand-crafted to a high standard of design, were expensive to produce and bought only by rich connoisseurs. He had an interest in Gothic shared by other reformers, such as the architects William Burges and Norman Shaw, and the three produced massive furniture in their own version of the Gothic manner.

JAPANESE INFLUENCES

A collection of Japanese objects at the 1862 International Exhibition in London opened the public's eye to the beauty of oriental goods. After this exhibition Arthur Liberty persuaded his retail employers (Farmer and Rogers) to open an oriental department. Later in 1875 he opened his own store, the famous Liberty shop in London's Regent Street to sell oriental goods.

'Art furniture' was an expression of this artistic revolt, known as the Aesthetic Movement. It was influenced by the interest in oriental design and the renewed interest in Georgian design which occurred at this time.

A major reformist, Charles Eastlake, in his book 'Hints on Household Taste in furniture, upholstery and other details' (1868), advocated cheap, simple rectangular furniture, panelled and boarded in the Gothic manner with pegged joints, no glue, staining, or french polishing and the minimum of decoration. He strongly influenced the Arts and Crafts Movement.

The architect E W Godwin produced the most original furniture of this time. Its keynote was functional simplicity. He

BUYING REPRODUCTIONS

☐ Some originals can still be found in antique shops – and even junk shops – at reasonable prices. However, don't be duped into buying an old reproduction in the belief that you're getting a priceless antique.

☐ Make sure the piece is well made – apart from beauty of form look for sturdy construction.

☐ Unless you want a piece simply as a focal point in a room, make sure it is suitable for its purpose. For instance, if you want a chest of drawers there is no point choosing an ornate chest with limited storage space.

☐ If you do buy a reproduction purely as decoration, be sure that it will look right in your home. Imposing Gothic pieces won't complement a small and homely living room!

☐ When buying reproductions from different periods, ensure they suit each other. A mix can be effective, while too many styles can simply look muddled.

used ebonized wood and rectilinear forms with tapering supports. His style of interior design appeared revolutionary – walls painted in light colours, plain undraped curtains, Japanese matting on the floor, a few Chinese pots, sparse furniture and a few simply framed paintings or etchings.

MATERIALS
Some of the most interesting furniture of the 19th century was experimental, using materials such as laminated and bent wood, papier-mâché, iron, wire, marble and horn. Papier-mâché was coated with layers of lacquer, decorated with gilt and multi-coloured paint, and inlaid with mother of pearl. Organic materials such as horn or tree branches were made up into rather surreal pieces of furniture for use in the garden, hall or conservatory.

In Austria, Michael Thonet invented a series of new processes for bending beechwood frames by treating them with heat and steam and produced the first bentwood chair, which was patented in 1874. The chair was made of three pieces of laminated wood. This process was not developed further until the 1930s.

Far-sighted designers experimented with metal. Casting processes had greatly improved and it was possible to cast large furniture components and fit them together with screws and braces. Highly original furniture was also made of wire, bent cold and twisted into elaborate shapes.

WALNUT VENEER CHEST OF DRAWERS
Style Chest showing the simple lines typical of Biedermeier furniture made in Austria and Germany. The beauty of the wood veneer is the main decorative element in many Biedermeier pieces, which represent the last stage of pre-industrial revolution design in Europe.

AUSTRIAN WALNUT CHAIR (c1820–25)
Style Another example of simple Biedermeier furniture where comfort is more important than style. The chair blends with 20th century furniture and could be used in almost any room.

'ELIZABETHAN' STYLE CHAIR (c1845)
Style In the so-called 'Elizabethan' style, with barley-sugar twist turning. Note that English flowers (in the tent-stitching embroidery) are used rather than classical motifs.

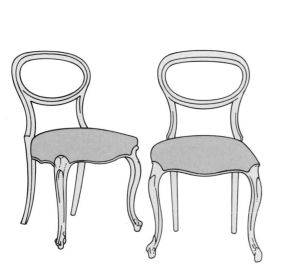

BALLOON-BACK CHAIRS IN ROSEWOOD
Style These chairs clearly show the rounding of forms typical of early Victorian furniture. Earlier versions of this chair had turned front legs but the cabriole legs popular from the 1850s are now considered to be more elegant. Fit as well into the modern drawing room as it did the Victorian. Particularly good as a dining or bedroom chair.

CARVED CHAIR (c1845)
Style An immense number and variety of chairs of this kind were produced, With their curvilinear outlines and Rococo details they form one of the basic types of naturalistic style. The low seat is also typical of this period.

HARRODS DRESSING TABLE (c1895)
Style A late Victorian reproduction of an early Victorian piece, showing characteristic rounding of forms and decoration. The many small drawers make it very practical.

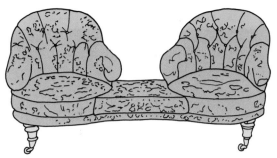

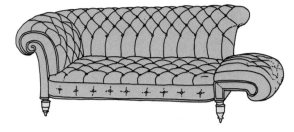

CHESTERFIELD SOFA
Style This chesterfield is know as the Ambidexter and is just one of many different styles of sofa that appeared in the mid 19th century. The ends can be adjusted to form a day bed. Chesterfields are still made today – usually in leather.

SOCIABLE TABLE (c1844)
Style Both chairs at each end of the table swivel round. Greater comfort is given by the deep sprung upholstery: the springs were covered with horsehair and cotton wadding which was held in place by deep buttoning.

GREAT EXHIBITION TABLE (c1851)
Style Made of carved walnut with a porcelain star inset in the top. The table illustrates the kind of over-indulgence of which some mid Victorian furniture makers were guilty. The naturalistic style has become Baroque in its fervour.

CARVED OAK DINING CHAIR
Style This strong design by Pugin, upholstered in imitation leather, shows that his love of Gothic did not make him follow Gothic models slavishly.

CABINET BY PUGIN (c1847)
Style Although the construction is straightforward, the elaborate carving is based on natural forms with a Gothic flavour.

CHAIR BY MORRIS & Co (c1865)
Style Based on a traditional Sussex cottage chair of turned wood, which is stained green and has a rush seat. This design was cheap and popular. It managed to fulfil Morris' aim of producing furniture for the average man more than any other piece produced by the firm.

SIDEBOARD (c1867)
Style In the Japanese manner and designed by E W Godwin. Made of ebonized wood with silver-plated fittings and inset panels of 'embossed leather' paper. Its functional simplicity excited much attention among members of the modern movement in the 1920s, particularly in Austria and Germany.

MEDIEVAL STYLE CABINET (c1860)
Style Designed by William Burges, a Gothic Revival architect. This imposing, if slightly absurd, piece was intended for use in the libraries of Gothic revival houses.

DRAWING ROOM CHIFFONIER
Style Designed by Charles Eastlake, this fairly simple piece is panelled and boarded in the Gothic manner with pegged joints. It is finished with the minimum of decoration – and manages to combine decorativeness and practicality.

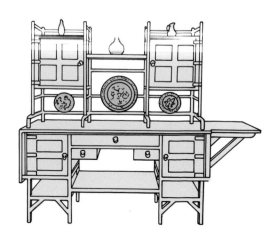

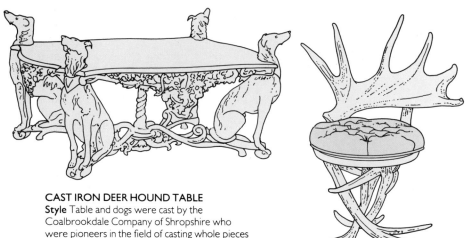

CAST IRON DEER HOUND TABLE

Style Table and dogs were cast by the Coalbrookdale Company of Shropshire who were pioneers in the field of casting whole pieces of furniture in iron. The dog collars bear the Hargreaves crest of the table's first owner.

CHAIR OF STAGS' ANTLERS
(Mid 19th century)

Style Like this chair, many eccentric pieces of furniture for country houses were made of antlers, roots of trees, and elephants' feet!

PAPIER-MÂCHÉ BED WITH BRASS MOUNT
(c1850)

Style Papier-mâché had little strength as a structural material – bed panels always had wood or metal inner structures. This bed is elaborately decorated in multi-coloured paint and inlaid with mother of pearl.

GARDEN SEAT (Late 19th century)

Style French garden seat made of welded iron rods, with a seat made of perforated sheet iron. Versions are still made today and are widely used in gardens or conservatories.

CAST IRON GARDEN SEAT (c1846)

Style Elaborate, cast iron English garden seat which became popular in America and was produced there until the end of the 19th century.

SWIVEL CHAIR (c1850)

Style Made by the American Spring Chair company, this chair has a spring mechanism. The style is a forerunner of the modern typist's chair.

ROCKING CHAIR (c1850)

Style English chair made of pieces of strap brass metal and upholstered in plush. Its restrained beauty is startlingly modern and anticipates the functionalism of the 1920s.

WICKER ROCKING CHAIR

Style Rocking chairs are an American invention. Earlier versions of this model were upholstered. In England, rocking chairs were seen as a novelty.

MICHAEL THONET'S CHAIR No 14

Style The most popular of Thonet's designs, this chair was made of bentwood with a cane seat and consisted of only six machine-made parts. The style is still made today.

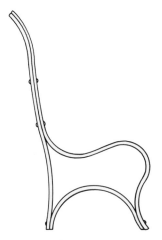

AMERICAN BENTWOOD CHAIR
(1874)

Style Side view of an American bent plywood chair made of three pieces of laminated wood. This technique was much exploited during the 1930s.

Twentieth Century Furniture

ARTS AND CRAFTS

The last 20 years of the 19th century witnessed a proliferation of Arts and Crafts groups, formed by designers who realized that little reform could be achieved by individuals working alone.

Most 'Art' furniture was commercially made (see Victorian Furniture) but Arts and Crafts designers, following the precepts of John Ruskin and William Morris, advocated a return to joiner-made furniture and chose to ignore all new technology. Most of these groups adopted the medieval title of 'guild'. The first was the Century Guild, founded in 1882 by the architect A H Mackmurdo. This guild, unlike those which followed, employed professional cabinet-makers for its furniture designs. Mackmurdo's own furniture, although not original in form, incorporated flame-like and waving plant motifs which represented the forerunners of Art Nouveau design.

An important figure in the movement was Charles Robert Ashbee, founder of the Guild of Handicraft. With fifty workmen, he aimed to recreate the working conditions of a medieval guild producing fine metalwork, jewellery, pottery and furniture. The guild gained international fame and the Grand Duke of Hesse invited its members to make furnishings (designed by M H Baillie Scott) for his palace in Darmstadt.

Another man much admired on the continent was the architect Charles Voysey. His furniture, with its simple forms and long thin shafts supporting the cabinets, shows the influence of Japanese design.

Three other architects, the brothers Sidney and Ernest Barnsley and Ernest Gimson, formed a group of craftsmen who produced furniture in the English tradition using indigenous woods: oak, elm, walnut and ash. The furniture was superbly made with fine detailing, and inspired a number of young 20th century designers like Ambrose Heal and Gordon Russell.

MAHOGANY CHAIR (c1882)
Style Mahogany chair with painted fretwork back designed by A H Mackmurdo. This piece boasts original Art Nouveau decoration on a very conservative shape.

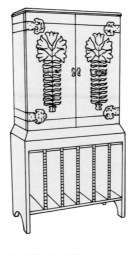

MUSIC CABINET (c1898)
Style Painted music cabinet designed by M H Baillie Scott and made by the Guild of Handicraft for the Palace of Darmstadt. Notice the elaborate decorative hinges.

WRITING DESK (c1896)
Style Oak writing desk by C F A Voysey. The simple form is enhanced by brass fittings and hinges.

OAK DRESSER
Style An oak dresser designed by Sidney Barnsley for his own cottage and made using only traditional methods. Typical of Barnsley's style, the chest is well-constructed to a simple design.

TACKLE CABINET
Style A walnut cabinet for storing fishing tackle by Ernest Gimson. The beauty of the wood was particularly noticeable in Gimson's work.

ART NOUVEAU

During the 1890s the Art Nouveau style swept rapidly through both Europe and America. Although seen as a revolt against earlier historically-inspired styles, its forms were still indebted to Rococo, Japanese and Celtic art. The term Art Nouveau stems from the name of a shop – 'L'Art Nouveau' – opened by Samuel Bing in Paris in 1895, which became an influential centre of art.

In was in France and Belgium that Art Nouveau was seen in its most flamboyant form. In france, Emile Gallé and Louis Majorelle took their inspiration straight from nature and used sinuous lines reminiscent of the growing limbs of trees and plants as well as butterfly, dragonfly and flower motifs. Hector Guimard, a Parisian architect/decorator, designed all the fittings, decorations and furniture for his houses. His furniture designs often posed severe problems for the cabinet-makers whose task it was to interpret and actually make the designs.

In Belgium, Van der Velde (who worked for Bing) placed less importance on decoration than on sweeping, flowing lines. Art Nouveau reached its peak in the work of another outstanding Belgian, Victor Horta, whose houses in Brussels were unique. Horta also designed all the furniture and fittings of the Hotel Solvay in Brussels to blend with the sinuous decoration which flowed over walls, floors and ceilings.

Full-blown European Art Nouveau received only limited appreciation in Britain. The work of the Scotsman Charles Rennie Mackintosh is sophisticated and restrained in comparison. His long attenuated furniture was usually painted in light colours with flowing linear decoration. His later rectilinear work was influential abroad.

The flowering of Art Nouveau was short-lived. Its flowing lines and subtle, delicate forms were poorly suited to mass, machine production: the best pieces were all hand-crafted and consequently expensive.

EMILE GALLÉ SIDEBOARD (c1903)
Style The structural supports on this sideboard are modelled on the stems of plants to create the impression that this piece of furniture is growing up from its roots. The ripe heads of wheat sheaves in the decoration are symbols of life.

MARQUETRY BUFFET
Style Marquetry buffet designed by Louis Majorelle. Note the marquetry of plump rabbits and snails nestling among intricately worked leaves.

LADDERBACK CHAIR
Style Chair with high back by the distinguished Scottish designer, Charles Rennie Mackintosh. Notice how refined the piece is in comparison with the European interpretations of Art Nouveau furniture.

VAN DER VELDE ARMCHAIR (c1898)
Style Armchair of Burmese sandalwood designed by Van der Velde. Upholstered in cotton batik. Note the flowing forms.

FURNITURE SUITE (c1898)
Style Suite of furniture intended for use in the drawing room, made in sycamore and upholstered in velvet. This suite was designed by Victor Horta for his own house. Horta's work was meant for the less ostentatious middle classes and this is one of his most successful suites.

THE MODERN MOVEMENT

Although Britain had prepared much of the groundwork in design for the Modern Movement, by the turn of the century the initiative passed to the continent. After the First World War, many of the surviving young people were filled with a hatred for war and its consequences. They wanted to change completely their lives and surroundings so there was a strong desire for experiment and change, particularly in Holland, Germany and France. In the early part of the century, artists had become interested in tribal art and the ensuing Cubist movement grew out of a belief that art and design should be cut down to the bare essentials.

The Dutch architect, Gerrit Rietveld, stripped furniture down to its basic forms and rethought the function of each piece. His work was brutally simple, painted in primary colours. Although easy to make and cheap, it was much too basic for traditional manufacturers and none of his designs was taken up commercially (although they have been made recently).

The basic ideas of Rietveld and others like him (who formed an avant garde group and expressed their ideas in a magazine called De Stijl) were considered and absorbed by a new design school which was founded by Walter Gropius in Germany and called the Bauhaus. This new school aimed to tackle the problems of designing for industry. Bauhaus' industrial design students were trained to combine all the talents of craftsmen, artists and designers. They were taught to abandon past styles and examine each design problem for a functional solution, choosing the most suitable material and technique. Consequently, former styles were discarded and the resulting Bauhaus furniture received international recognition.

The most characteristic piece of Bauhaus furniture, the tubular steel cantilevered chair, introduced a see-through element into furniture design. Designed by Marcel Breuer, the chair became the prototype for many versions over the years – it had beauty and comfort and used the minimum of materials, labour and cost.

The Thonet firm was a large organization which exported bentwood furniture to many parts of the world. It progressed from bending wood to bending metal, and countless pieces of metal furniture were made for schools and other public buildings, but few people wanted it in their homes.

The invention of latex foam (from experiments in the motor industry in 1928) brought more changes. Upholstery units could be moulded in one operation, either in the form of loose cushions or pre-formed units which were then bonded to the chair frame.

In France, Le Corbusier and Charlotte Perriand were experimenting along similar lines to the Germans. Apart from his famous chaise longue, Corbusier's most striking contribution to furniture design was his 'Grand Confort' armchair designed in the form of a cube. Contrary to tradition, its framework of chromium-plated steel tubing was on the outside, like a cage which supported four large loose cushions to form seat, back and sides.

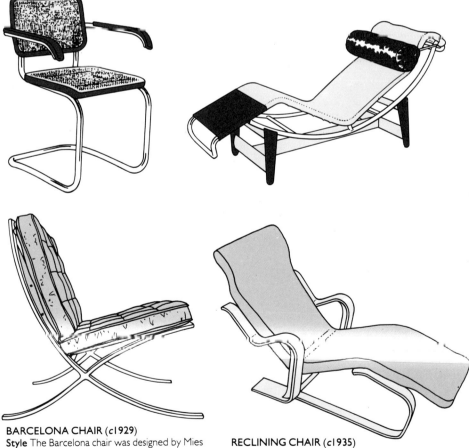

CANTILEVERED CHAIR (c1928)
Style The Cesca cantilevered chair by Marcel Breuer had a chromium-plated tubular steel frame, cane back and seat. Still produced today.

CHAISE LONGUE (c1928)
Style Adjustable chaise longue with headrest. Made of chromium-plated, tubular steel on an opaque, black steel base. Designed by Le Corbusier in association with Charlotte Perriand and Pierre Jeanneret, this chaise longue is still made today.

GRAND CONFORT CHAIR (c1928)
Style The Grand Confort chair by Le Corbusier has not lost any of its design appeal over the years and its bulky, square shape is comfortable and can look good in a modern, smart setting. The chromium-plated, tubular steel frame supports loose upholstered cushions. Still produced today.

BARCELONA CHAIR (c1929)
Style The Barcelona chair was designed by Mies Van der Rohe in 1929. Crossing, solid stainless steel bars form the frame which supports the leather-covered cushions. This sophisticated chair – which is still in production – has deceptively simple curves.

RECLINING CHAIR (c1935)
Style Reclining chair (and matching occasional table) in bent birchwood designed by Marcel Breuer after he had moved to Britain. Latex foam seat and back. A very comfortable and distinctive piece for a living room. Still in production.

In the 1930s, many designers began to experiment with plywood and laminated birchwood, both cheap and plentiful materials. The Finn Alvar Aalto was the first to exploit these woods. He experimented with the various different ways of moulding plywood and, with his wife Aino, Aalto started the Helsinki firm of Artek in 1933 to manufacture his experimental designs. Artek continued to develop its techniques and the company manufactured shelf unit brackets, tables, stools and chairs.

The Scandinavians came late to industrialization and were thus able to avoid the cheap, shoddy, manufactured furniture that other countries suffered. By the 1930s they had adapted to the new technology and production methods and are still producing functional and pleasing furniture without sacrificing their high standards.

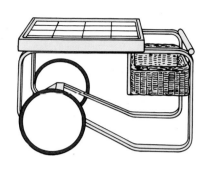

ALVAR AALTO TROLLEY (c1936)
Style Tea trolley designed for the Artek company. Since it was first produced it has remained in continuous production. Made of bent laminated wood, the trolley's functionality and elegant simplicity is typical of Aalto's designs.

ALVAR AALTO CHAIR
Style Cantilevered armchair by Alvar Aalto. Birch laminated frame with pre-formed plywood seat and back made from a single piece.

ART DECO

The Art Deco style stands quite apart from the work of the progressive designers. Though it started to evolve around 1910, it took its name from the Paris Exhibition of Decorative and Industrial Arts of 1925, when the style was, in fact, already past its best. The furniture forms are severe, with smooth surfaces to accentuate the extravagant materials used: wood chosen for its distinctive markings, ebony, ivory, lacquer, glass, leather, tortoiseshell, sharkskin and mother of pearl. An oriental influence, inspired by the famous Ballet Russe, introduced strong, vibrant colours and a general lowering of seating.

The new coffee table, low in height, was often oriental in character. Favourite motifs were swags and baskets of stylized flowers, stylized fountain and tree forms and geometric patterns.

The best furniture, as exemplified in the work of Emile Jacques Ruhlmann, was of a very high technical standard. Unfortunately, however, popular mass-produced Art Deco fed on a variety of very disparate sources: Cubism, Oriental and African art, Aztec and Egyptian influences as well as Futuristic images of speed and a general rounding of forms.

But Heal and Son was probably the only large, well-established furnishing house to take an interest in contemporary design. It was run by Ambrose Heal, a talented designer himself, who gathered other decorators and furniture designers around him. In the 1920s and 30s they sold not only good quality hand-crafted furniture, but also modern continental tubular steel and laminated wood furniture. They also produced 'series' furniture made with traditional methods and materials but using factory methods for mechanical processes like sawing and planing.

Gordon Russell was another furniture-maker who made high quality furniture using factory methods of production, as well as hand-crafted pieces.

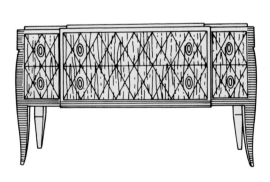

IVORY CHEST OF DRAWERS (c1924)
Style A chest of drawers by Emile Jacques Ruhlmann. Veneered in Macassar ebony with inlaid lines of ivory, and ivory handles. The tapered legs are typical of Ruhlmann's furniture. A collector's piece.

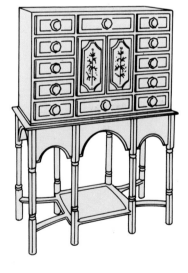

RUSSELL CABINET
Style Cabinet designed by Gordon Russell. Made from solid English walnut inlaid with ebony and yew. The handles are in ebony and laburnum.

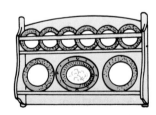

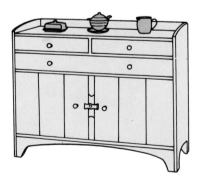

OAK DRESSER
Style Unpolished oak dresser and plate rack by Ambrose Heal. A simple well-made piece in traditional English style.

POST WAR DESIGN

Scandinavia, the United States and Italy have dominated furniture design since the war. Scandinavian production was hardly halted by the war years and their designs were fresh and exciting to the rest of Europe in the 1950s.

The introduction of plastics brought about one of the greatest changes in furniture design. The war-time need for lightweight malleable materials which could support considerable weight produced a plastic which could be adapted to furniture making, and the exciting shapes that designers had striven for in the 1920s and 30s became possible. Gropius, Breuer and other members of the Bauhaus who had fled Nazi Germany in the 1930s were teaching in the USA and exerted considerable influence on design trends.

A native American, Charles Eames, came to the fore at this time with his experiments with shell forms. At first he used sheet metal stamped out in a shell shape to form seat, back and arms in one piece. Later he tried a new material, polyester reinforced with glass fibre (GRP), for his famous DAR chair. Some very exciting designs were produced in this material by eminent designers – for example, the tulip pedestal and side chairs of Eero Saarinen (1956) and the elegant fluid swan and egg chairs designed by the Dane, Arne Jacobsen in 1958. Unfortunately, these beautiful chairs were expensive to produce because of the high costs of tooling up and materials. It was not until a very tough plastic, polypropylene, was discovered in Britain that it became possible to make furniture by injection moulding for half the cost of GRP. The first polypropylene chair was designed by Robin Day for the Hille firm in 1963.

Italian design, which came to the fore in the 1960s, had great panache but is difficult to classify because of its variety. New techniques and materials – plastics, laminated wood and plywood – were used with great imagination in an attempt to produce cheap, well-designed furniture for everyone. Less permanent furniture such as the Sacco and the Blow chairs come into this category. Lacquer was a favourite finish and bold use was made of colour.

British design had become rather provincial. When Terence Conran opened his first Habitat shops in 1964 he aimed to make well-designed furniture – ranging from kitchen utensils, and pots and pans to fabrics and furniture – available to everyone. The basic concept was that absolutely everything sold in Habitat shops would mix and match happily in the middle class home.

At the top end of the market there has been a strong revival of fine craftsmanship. In England the workshops of designers such as John Makepeace are producing fine pieces which are impossible to make with a machine. The highly organic shapes created by Wendell Castle and Michael Coffey in the USA are also hand-crafted, but represent a more sculptural approach to furniture design.

EASY CHAIR (c1945)

Style Upholstered chair with lacquered and oiled teak frame designed by Finn Juhl. First shown at the Copenhagen Cabinet-Maker's Guild exhibition. Juhl was renowned for his sculptural use of wood.

BB CABINET

Style The Boligens Byggeskabe (BB Cabinet) was designed by the Danish architects Borge Mogensen and Grethe Meyer in 1957. The Danes were the first to experiment with interchangeable units which were flexible enough to be adapted to changing needs.

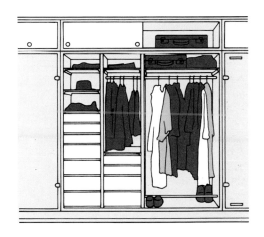

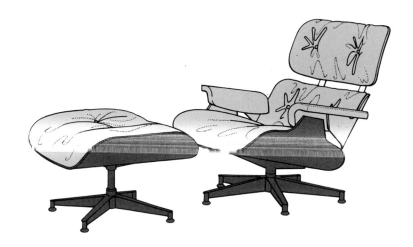

DAR CHAIR (c1949)

Style Designed by Charles Eames, it was the first chair with a seat of moulded glass fibre. Almost indestructible, it won't stain or scratch.

CHAIR AND OTTOMAN (c1956)

Style Lounge chair and ottoman by Charles Eames, made of moulded plywood shells which are veneered with rosewood. The cushions are filled with down, covered in leather and fastened to the shells. The chair swivels on an aluminium base. The matching ottoman is upholstered in the same fabric with a similar aluminium base.

One of Eames' more luxurious styles, the chair and ottoman combine comfort with masculine good looks.

TULIP CHAIR (c1956)
Style 'Tulip' pedestal chair and side chair by Eero Saarinen. It has a glass fibre shell and an aluminium base with a wool-covered seat. The pedestal is enamelled in white.

EGG CHAIR
Style The Egg chair by Arne Jacobsen was made from moulded glass fibre and covered in either leather or fabric. The chair swivels on a low, aluminium base. This and another chair by Jacobsen, the swan chair, are beautiful examples of the interesting experiments in moulded glass fibre that were being made in Scandinavia in the 1950s.

STACKING CHAIR (c1963)
Style Polypropylene stacking chair by Robin Day for Hille & Company. The stacking chair was the first injection-moulded polypropylene chair. The tube base can be coated with black nylon, black stove enamelled or bright chrome. Its main advantage is that it will not chip or discolour and it is washable.

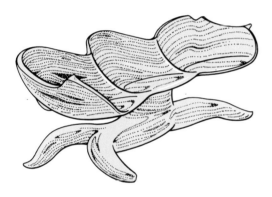

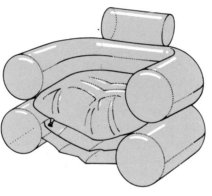

CHERRYWOOD SOFA
Style A laminated cherrywood, three-seater sofa made by the American designer Wendell Castle. This hand-crafted piece is a one-off but is a powerful example of the new interest that has emerged in sculptural forms in furniture.

BLOW CHAIR (c1967)
Style Blow chair by Scolari, D'Urbino, Lomazzi and De Pas, manufactured in PVC film. This chair was the first Italian mass-produced 'blow up' chair and was offered in four colours.

ROCKING CHAIR (c1967)
Style 'Dondolo' rocking chair made in three colours by Cesare Leonardi & Franca Stagi. A beautiful sculptural form made in moulded glass fibre. It is principally an exciting sculptural form and its role as something to sit on takes a secondary place.

ISOLA STORAGE UNITS
Style Habitat storage units available as either a low level unit (with three shelves) or in a high level version (five shelves). Made in solid wood and veneered in 'anegre', the wood uprights are painted black. One of the latest Habitat designs.

DESK FOR TWO
Style Desk for two people by the English furniture-maker, John Makepeace. Hand-crafted in solid Macassar ebony and English holly-wood. This is a unique piece managing to combine working areas with plenty of storage in a compact piece of furniture – there are six full-length drawers. Like all Makepeace's furniture, it is designed for a specific function.

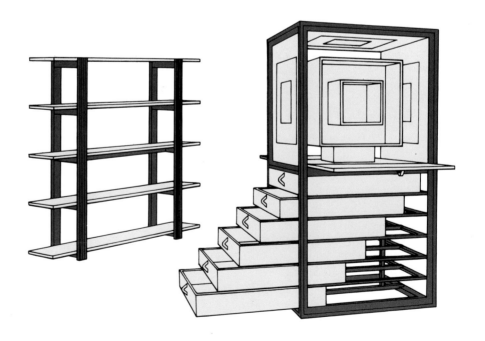

INDEX

PHOTOGRAPHIC CREDITS
1 Luxaflex Blinds, 2-3 EWA/Michael Dunne, 4-5 IKEA, 6 Habitat, 7 Next Interior, 8(tl) Next Interior, 8 (tr) Schreiber, 8(bl) Armitage Shanks, 8(br) Cover Plus with Woolworth, 9(t) National Magazine Co/David Montgomery, 9(b) Next Interior, 10 William Douglas/Eaglemoss, 11 Bruce Hemming/Eaglemoss, 12 Simon Butcher/Eaglemoss, 13 Syndication International, 14-15 Habitat, 14(b) Dulux, 15(tr) Allmilmö, 15(b) Syndication International, 16 William Douglas/Eaglemoss, 17, 18 Steve Tanner/Eaglemoss, 19 jaycee Furniture Ltd, 20(t) National Magazine Co/David Brittain, 20(bl) PWA International, 20(br) C.P. Hart, 21(t) National Magazine Co/Dennis Stone, 21(b) Marks and Spencer plc, 22(t) Coloroll, 22(b) Dulux Paints, 23 EWA/Michael Dunne, 24(t) EWA/Spike Powell, 24(b) Pipe Dreams, 25(t) EWA/Michael Dunne, 25(b) EWA/Clive Helm, 26 EWA/Michael Dunne, 27, 28 Steve Tanner/Eaglemoss, 29 Coles and Sons, 30(t) Designers Guild, 30(b) EWA/Michael Dunne, 31(tl) Arthur Sanderson and Sons, 31 (tr) Next Interior, 31(b) Arthur Sanderson and Sons, 32 Arthur Sanderson and Sons, 33, 34 Steve Tanner/Eaglemoss, 35 EWA, 36(t) EWA, 36(b) Osborne and Little, 37(tl) EWA/Michael Dunne, 37(tr) Bevan Furnell, 37(b) EWA/Michael Dunne, 38 PWA International, 39, 40 Steve Tanner/Eaglemoss, 41 Jalag, 42(t) Dulux Paints, 42(bl) EWA/Michael Nicholson, 42(br) EWA/Spike Powell, 43(t) Arthur Sanderson and Sons, 43(b) Camera Press, 44 William Douglas/Eaglemoss, 45 EWA/Andreas von Einsiedel, 46(t) Syndication International, 46(b) EWA, 47(tl) Hamilton Weston Wallpapers, 47(tr) EWA/Jerry Tubby, 47(b) EWA/Michael Dunne, 48 EWA, 49, 50 Di Lewis/Eaglemoss, 51 PWA International, 52(t) Osborne and Little, 52(b) Moben Kitchens, 53(t) Syndication International, 53(c) National Magazine Co/Spike Powell, 53(b) Dorma, 54 Dorma, 55, 56 Nelson Hargreaves/Eaglemoss, 57 PWA International, 58(t) Crown Wallcoverings, 58(b) EWA/Neil Lorimer, 59(t) Arthur Sanderson and Sons, 60 Crown Wallcoverings, 61, 62 Steve Tanner/Eaglemoss, 63 Syndication International, 64(tl) Cristal Tiles, 64(tr) Crown Paints, 64(b) EWA/Spike Powell, 65(t) Arcaid/Richard Bryant, 65(b) Magnet and Southern, 66 EWA/Spike Powell, 67, 68 Di Lewis/Eaglemoss, 69 Mondadoripress, 70 Cassina Ltd, 70(b) National Magazine Co/Jan Baldwin, 70-1 Cassina Ltd, 71(b) SieMatic, 72 Mondadoripress, 73, 74 Di Lewis/Eaglemoss, 75 Syndication International, 76(t) Camera Press, 76(b) Jalag, 77(t) Hulsta, 77(bl) Wickes and Co, 77(br) Hulsta, 78 Hulsta.

Front cover: (tl) Jewels of India range by Crowsons Fabrics, Crowson House, Bellbrook Park, Uckfield, East Sussex, TN22 1QZ. Tel: 01825 761044; (tr) Dulux Paints. Tel: 01420 23024 for stockist information; (bl) Harlequin Fabrics and Wallcoverings, Cossington Road, Sileby, Loughborough LE12 7RU. Tel: 01509 813112; (br) ICI Paints. Tel: 01420 23024 for stockist information.
(EWA - Elizabeth Whiting and Associates)